Quod scriptura, non iubet vetat

The Latin translates, "What is not commanded in scripture, is forbidden:'

On the Cover: Baptists rejoice to hold in common with other evangelicals the main principles of the orthodox Christian faith. However, there are points of difference and these differences are significant. In fact, because these differences arise out of God's revealed will, they are of vital importance. Hence, the barriers of separation between Baptists and others can hardly be considered a trifling matter. To suppose that Baptists are kept apart solely by their views on Baptism or the Lord's Supper is a regrettable misunderstanding. Baptists hold views which distinguish them from Catholics, Congregationalists, Episcopalians, Lutherans, Methodists, Pentecostals, and Presbyterians, and the differences are so great as not only to justify, but to demand, the separate denominational existence of Baptists. Some people think Baptists ought not teach and emphasize their differences but as E.J. Forrester stated in 1893, "Any denomination that has views which justify its separate existence, is bound to promulgate those views. If those views are of sufficient importance to justify a separate existence, they are important enough to create a duty for their promulgation ... the very same reasons which justify the separate existence of any denomination make it the duty of that denomination to teach the distinctive doctrines upon which its separate existence rests." If Baptists have a right to a separate denominational life, it is their duty to propagate their distinctive principles, without which their separate life cannot be justified or maintained.

Many among today's professing Baptists have an agenda to revise the Baptist distinctives and redefine what it means to be a Baptist. Others don't understand why it even matters. The books being reproduced in the *Baptist Distinctives Series* are republished in order that Baptists from the past may state, explain and defend the primary Baptist distinctives as they understood them. It is hoped that this Series will provide a more thorough historical perspective on what it means to be distinctively Baptist.

The Lord Jesus Christ asked, *"And why call ye me, Lord, Lord, and do not the things which I say?"* (Luke 6:46). The immediate context surrounding this question explains what it means to be a true disciple of Christ. Addressing the same issue, Christ's question is meant to show that a confession of discipleship to the Lord Jesus Christ is inconsistent and untrue if it is not accompanied with a corresponding submission to His authoritative commands. Christ's question teaches us that a true recognition of His authority as Lord inevitably includes a submission to the authority of His Word. Hence, with this question Christ has made it forever impossible to separate His authority as King from the authority of His Word. These two principles—the authority of Christ as King and the authority of His Word—are the two most fundamental Baptist distinctives. The first gives rise to the second and out of these two all the other Baptist distinctives emanate. As F.M. Iams wrote in 1894, "Loyalty to Christ as King, manifesting itself in a constant and unswerving obedience to His will as revealed in His written Word, is the real source of all the Baptist distinctives:' In the search for the *primary* Baptist distinctive many have settled on the Lordship of Christ as the most basic distinctive. Strangely, in doing this, some have attempted to separate Christ's Lordship from the authority of Scripture, as if you could embrace Christ's authority without submitting to what He commanded. However, while Christ's Lordship and Kingly authority can be isolated and considered essentially for discussion's sake, we see from Christ's own words in Luke 6:46 that His Lordship is really inseparable from His Word and, with regard to real Christian discipleship, there can be no practical submission to the one without a practical submission to the other.

In the symbol above the Kingly Crown and the Open Bible represent the inseparable truths of Christ's Kingly and Biblical authority. The Crown and Bible graphics are supplemented by three Bible verses (Ecclesiastes 8:4, Matthew 28:18-20, and Luke 6:46) that reiterate and reinforce the inextricable connection between the authority of Christ as King and the authority of His Word. The truths symbolized by these components are further emphasized by the Latin quotation - *quod scriptura, non iubet vetat*— i.e., "What is not commanded in scripture, is forbidden:' This Latin quote has been considered historically as a summary statement of the regulative principle of Scripture. Together these various symbolic components converge to exhibit the two most foundational Baptist Distinctives out of which all the other Baptist Distinctives arise. Consequently, we have chosen this composite symbol as a logo to represent the primary truths set forth in the *Baptist Distinctives Series*.

DISTINCTIVE PRINCIPLES
OF
BAPTISTS

JAMES MADISON PENDLETON
(1811-1891)

DISTINCTIVE PRINCIPLES

OF

BAPTISTS

BY

J. M. PENDLETON

With a Biographical Sketch of the Author by John Franklin Jones

PHILADELPHIA:
AMERICAN BAPTIST PUBLICATION SOCIETY
1420 CHESTNUT STREET.
1882

Reprinted 2006

by

THE BAPTIST STANDARD BEARER, INC.
No. 1 Iron Oaks Drive
Paris, Arkansas 72855
(479) 963-3831

THE WALDENSIAN EMBLEM
lux lucet in tenebris
"The Light Shineth in the Darkness"

ISBN# 1579785441

TO

THE BAPTIST BROTHERHOOD.

THIS VOLUME

(WRITTEN IN ADVOCACY OF PRINCIPLES WHICH DISTINGUISH
THEM FROM OTHER RELIGIOUS DENOMINATIONS)

IS

Respectfully and Affectionately Dedicated

BY

THE AUTHOR.

CONTENTS.

CHAPTER I.

                                                      PAGE

BAPTISTS REGARD THE BAPTISM OF UNCONSCIOUS INFANTS AS UNSCRIPTURAL, AND INSIST ON THE BAPTISM OF BELIEVERS IN CHRIST; AND OF BELIEVERS ALONE......... 11

SECTION I.

The account given of John's baptism and of the personal ministry of Christ affords no justification of infant baptism............ 13

SECTION II.

The Commission given by the Saviour to his apostles just before his ascension to heaven furnishes no plea for infant baptism............ 17

SECTION III.

There is no instance of infant baptism on the day of Pentecost, nor in Samaria under the preaching of Philip........ 21

SECTION IV.

The argument from household baptisms in favor of infant baptism is invalid 25

SECTION V.

Certain passages in the New Testament supposed by some Pedobaptists to refer to infant baptism shown to have no such reference.. 30

SECTION VI.

The allusions to baptism in the Apostolic Epistles forbid the supposition that infants were baptized........................... 33

SECTION VII.

The argument from the supposed identity of the Jewish Commonwealth and the gospel church of no force.................... 39

SECTION VIII.

The argument from circumcision fails................................. 63

SECTION IX.

The historical argument examined...................................... 72

SECTION X.

Objections to infant baptism... 80

CHAPTER II.

BAPTISTS CONSIDER THE IMMERSION IN WATER OF A BELIEVER IN CHRIST ESSENTIAL TO BAPTISM—SO ESSENTIAL THAT WITHOUT IT THERE IS NO BAPTISM...................... 90

CONTENTS.

SECTION I.
Greek lexicons give "immerse," "dip," or "plunge" as the primary and ordinary meaning of *baptizo* 90

SECTION II.
Distinguished Pedobaptist scholars and theologians admit that *baptizo* means "to immerse" 98

SECTION III.
The classical usage of *baptizo* establishes the position of Baptists 104

SECTION IV.
The design of baptism furnishes an argument in favor of the position of Baptists 113

SECTION V.
The places selected for the administration of baptism, and circumstances attending its administration, as referred to in the New Testament, supply an additional argument in proof of the position of Baptists 121

SECTION VI.
History bears testimony to the practice of immersion, except in cases of sickness and urgent necessity, for more than thirteen hundred years 135

SECTION VII.
Pedobaptist objections answered 147

CHAPTER III.

BAPTISTS HOLD THAT, ACCORDING TO THE SCRIPTURAL ORDER, PERSONS MUST COME FIRST TO CHRIST, AND THEN TO THE CHURCH AND ITS ORDINANCES.......................... 159

SECTION I.
The doctrine of baptismal regeneration reverses this order..... 160

SECTION II.
The practice of infant baptism reverses this order................ 164

CHAPTER IV.

BAPTISTS BELIEVE THAT A SCRIPTURAL CHURCH IS A LOCAL CONGREGATION OF BAPTIZED BELIEVERS INDEPENDENT, UNDER CHRIST, OF THE STATE AND OF EVERY OTHER CHURCH, HAVING IN ITSELF AUTHORITY TO DO WHATEVER A CHURCH CAN OF RIGHT DO............................ 169

SECTION I.
A scriptural church a local congregation of baptized believers.. 170

SECTION II.
The Lord's Supper observed by local churches..................... 174

SECTION III.
Definition of church independence...................................... 182

SECTION IV.
The churches of the New Testament received, excluded, and restored members... 190

CONTENTS.

SECTION V.
PAGE
The churches of the New Testament appointed their officers.. 195

SECTION VI.
Church action is final.. 205

SECTION VII.
Superior advantages of Independency............................ 211

CONCLUSION.. 224

INDEX... 233

INDEX OF SCRIPTURES....................................... 237

DISTINCTIVE PRINCIPLES

OF

BAPTISTS.

CHAPTER I.

BAPTISTS REGARD THE BAPTISM OF UNCONSCIOUS INFANTS AS UNSCRIPTURAL, AND INSIST ON THE BAPTISM OF BELIEVERS IN CHRIST; AND OF BELIEVERS ALONE.

BEFORE showing wherein Baptists differ from other Christian denominations, it may be well for me to say that in many things there is substantial agreement.

As to the inspiration, and the consequent infallibility, of the word of God, there is no difference of opinion. The Bible is recognized as the supreme standard of faith and practice—that is to say, it teaches us what to believe and what to do.

Salvation by grace is a doctrine which commands the cordial assent of all Christians. While "sin reigns unto death," they rejoice that "grace reigns through righteousness unto eternal life by Jesus Christ our Lord." They expect through endless ages to ascribe their salvation to the sovereign grace of God.

Justification by faith in Christ is a fundamental article of belief among all Christians. Acceptance with God on the ground of their works they know to be impossible, and they give the Lord Jesus the trustful reception which the gospel claims for him, and of which his person, character, and mediatorial work render him infinitely worthy. Christ is the object of their faith.

Regeneration by the Holy Spirit is a Christian doctrine. To be "born of the Spirit" is an essential part of salvation; for the subjects of this second birth become the children of God and heirs of heaven. They "put on the new man, which after God is created in righteousness and true holiness."

With regard to these and kindred topics Baptists are in accord with other evangelical Christians; but there are points of difference. On these points Baptists hold views which distinguish them from Presbyterians, Episcopalians, Congregationalists, Lutherans, Methodists. These views they deem so important as to justify their denominational existence; and because they hold these views they are a people "everywhere spoken against." If, however, the distinctive principles of Baptists have their foundation in the word of God, they should be not only earnestly espoused, but maintained with unswerving fidelity. No truth taught in the Scriptures can be considered unimportant while the words of Jesus are remembered: "Whosoever therefore shall break one of these least commandments, and shall teach men so, he shall be called the least in the kingdom of heaven: but whosoever shall do and teach them, the same shall be called great in the kingdom of heaven" (Matt. v. 19); "Teaching them to observe all things whatsoever I have commanded you" (Matt. xxviii. 20).

SECTION I.

The account given of John's baptism and of the personal ministry of Christ affords no justification of infant baptism.

In the third chapter of Matthew it is thus written: "In those days came John the Baptist, preaching in the wilderness of Judea, and saying, Repent ye: for the kingdom of heaven is at hand. . . . Then went out to him Jerusalem, and all Judea, and all the region round about Jordan, and were baptized of him in Jordan, confessing their sins. But when he saw many of the Pharisees and Sadducees come to his baptism, he said unto them, O generation of vipers, who hath warned you to flee from the wrath to come? Bring forth therefore fruits meet for repentance: and think not to say within yourselves, We have Abraham to our father: for I say unto you, that God is able of these stones to raise up children unto Abraham."

From these verses we learn that John preached repentance; that those whom he baptized confessed their sins; and that descent from Abraham was not a qualification for baptism. There is nothing in the narrative that can suggest the idea of the baptism of impenitent adults or of unconscious infants. This is equally true of the account of John's ministry as given by the other three evangelists.

Paul, in explaining John's baptism, says, "John verily baptized with the baptism of repentance, saying unto the people, that they should believe on him which should come after him, that is, on Christ Jesus" (Acts xix. 4). Here it is plain that John required in those he baptized repentance and faith. They were not only to repent, but to believe in the coming Christ, for whom it was John's mission to "prepare a people." There is not the remotest allusion to the baptism of any who either did not or could not repent and believe in Christ. Baptists, so far as the subjects of baptism are concerned, certainly imitate closely the example of John the Baptist.

The disciples of Christ baptized no infants during

his ministry. The only reference we have to the baptisms administered by them before the Redeemer's death and resurrection is in John iii. 26; iv. 1, 2, as follows: "And they came unto John, and said unto him, Rabbi, he that was with thee beyond Jordan, to whom thou bearest witness, behold, the same baptizeth, and all men come to him;" "When therefore the Lord knew how the Pharisees had heard that Jesus made and baptized more disciples than John, though Jesus himself baptized not, but his disciples." From the words quoted from the third chapter it would be thought that Jesus baptized personally; but we have an explanation of the matter in the language of the fourth chapter. Baptism was not administered by the Saviour; but, as his apostles acted under his authority, he is represented as doing what they did by his direction. The fact, however, which deserves special notice is "that Jesus made and baptized more disciples than John." There is a distinction between *making* and *baptizing* disciples. First in order was the process of discipleship to Christ, and then baptism as a recognition of discipleship. Could unconscious infants be made disciples? Manifestly not. Then, according to this passage, they were not eligible to baptism; for the inference is irresistible that none were baptized who had not first been made disciples.

The oft-repeated verse, "Suffer little children, and forbid them not, to come unto me: for of such is the kingdom of heaven," does not justify infant baptism. For what purpose were these children taken to Christ? That he should baptize them? Evidently not; for *he* did not baptize. Were they taken to him that his disciples might baptize them? If so, it is marvellous that the disciples rebuked those who had charge of them. The preceding verse shows why these children were taken to Christ: "Then were brought unto him little children, that he should put his hands on them and pray: and the disciples rebuked them" (Matt. xix. 13). There was a specific object in view. It was not that the "little children" might be baptized, but that the Saviour might put his hands on them and pray. Who has the right to infer that these children were baptized, or that baptism was mentioned in their presence? The sacred narrative is silent on the subject; and it may be said with positive certainty that the New Testament, from the birth of John the Baptist to the death of Christ, says nothing concerning infant baptism. If, however, Pedobaptists should admit this, they would still insist—many of them, at least—that there is authority for their practice bearing date subsequent to the Redeemer's death and resurrection. We shall see whether there is such authority.

SECTION II.

The Commission given by the Saviour to his apostles just before his ascension to heaven furnishes no plea for infant baptism.

The circumstances connected with the giving of this Commission were replete with interest. The Lord Jesus had finished the work which he came down from heaven to accomplish. He had offered himself a sacrifice for sin. He had exhausted the cup of atoning sorrow. He had lain in the dark mansions of the grave. He had risen in triumph from the dead, and was about to ascend to the right hand of the Majesty on high. Invested with perfect mediatorial authority, he said to his apostles, "All power is given unto me in heaven and in earth. Go ye therefore and teach all nations, baptizing them in the name of the Father, and of the Son, and of the Holy Ghost; teaching them to observe all things whatsoever I have commanded you: and, lo, I am with you alway, even unto the end of the world. Amen." Mark records the same Commission thus: "Go ye into all the world and preach the gospel to every creature. He that believeth and is baptized shall be saved; but he that believeth not shall be damned." Luke's record is this: "Thus it is written, and thus it behooved Christ to suffer, and to rise from the dead the third day; and that repentance and remission of sins should be preached in his name among all nations, beginning at Jerusalem" (Matt. xxviii. 18, 19, 20; Mark xvi. 15, 16; Luke xxiv. 46, 47).

Surely the language of this Commission is plain. Matthew informs us that teaching—or making disciples; for the Greek verb means "to disciple" or "to make disciples"—is to precede baptism, Mark establishes the priority of faith to baptism, and Luke connects repentance and remission of sins with the execution of the Commission. No man can, in obedience to this Commission, baptize either an unbeliever or an infant. The unbeliever is not a penitent disciple, and it is impossible for an infant to repent and believe the gospel.

It may be laid down as a principle of common sense which commends itself to every unprejudiced mind that *a commission to do a thing or things authorizes only the doing of the thing or things specified in it.* The doing of all other things is virtually forbidden. There is a maxim of law: *Expressio unius est exclusio alterius.** It must be so; for otherwise there could be no definiteness in contracts between men, and no precision in either the enactments of legislative bodies or in the decrees of courts of justice. This maxim may be illustrated in a thousand ways. Numerous scriptural

---

* "The expression of one thing is the exclusion of another."

illustrations are at hand; I will name a few. God commanded Noah to build an ark of *gopher-wood*. He assigns no reason why gopher-wood should be used. The command, however, is positive, and it forbids the use of any other kind of wood for that purpose. Abraham was commanded to offer his son Isaac for a burnt-offering. He was virtually forbidden to offer any other member of his family. Ay, more, he could not offer an animal till the original order was revoked by him who gave it, and a second order was given requiring the sacrifice of a ram in the place of Isaac. The institution of the passover furnishes a striking illustration, or rather a series of illustrations. A lamb was to be killed—not a heifer; it was to be of the first year—not of the second or third; a male—not a female; without blemish—not with blemish; on the fourteenth day of the month—not on some other day; the blood to be applied to the door-posts and lintels—not elsewhere. These illustrations are all scriptural, but I may refer also to the Constitution of the United States. It says of the President: "He shall have power, by and with the advice and consent of the Senate, to make treaties, provided two-thirds of the senators present concur." This language in effect forbids the making of a treaty by the President alone, or by the President and the House of Representatives in Congress, or by the

President and the Supreme Court. It pronounces invalid a treaty made by the President and a majority of "senators present," for there must be "two-thirds." The Constitution declares that the House of Representatives "shall have the sole power of impeachment," and the Senate "shall have the sole power to try all impeachments." Here the Senate is as effectually inhibited from the "power of impeachment" as is the House of Representatives from the power of trying "impeachments." Neither the President, the Supreme Court, nor the Senate can impeach, but the House of Representatives alone. The President, the Supreme Court, and the House of Representatives combined cannot "try impeachments," but the Senate alone.

In application of the principle laid down and of the law-maxim illustrated, I affirm that the Commission of Christ to the apostles, in requiring them to baptize disciples—believers—forbids, in effect, the baptism of all others. It will not do to say that we are not forbidden in so many words to baptize infants. The same may be said of unbelievers, and even of horses and sheep and bells.

This examination of the Commission fully authorizes me to say that it furnishes no plea for infant baptism. But it will be said—for it has been said a thousand times—that if infants are not to be baptized because they cannot believe, they cannot, for the same reason, be saved. If the salvation of infants depends on their faith, they cannot be saved. They are incapable of faith. They are doubtless saved through the mediation of Jesus Christ, but it is not by faith. The opponents of Baptists signally fail to accomplish their purpose in urging this objection to our views. They intend to make us concede the propriety of infant baptism or force us to a denial of infant salvation. But we make neither the concession nor the denial. As soon as we say that infants are not saved by faith, but without faith, their objection is met and demolished.

SECTION III.

There is no instance of infant baptism on the day of Pentecost, nor in Samaria under the preaching of Philip.

The day of Pentecost was a memorable day. Forty days after his resurrection Jesus had ascended to heaven. Before his ascension, however, he gave his apostles express command to tarry at Jerusalem till endued with power from on high. This power was received, in connection with their baptism in the Holy Spirit, on the day of Pentecost. They were copiously imbued with the Spirit—placed more fully under his influence than ever before. All things whatsoever Jesus had said to them were brought to their remembrance. They were required for the first time to show their understanding of the Commission of their ascended Lord. How did they understand it? How did they execute it? First, the gospel was preached. Peter in his great sermon proved Jesus to be the Christ, and derived his proof from the Old-Testament Scriptures. Then he charged his hearers with the crime of crucifying the Lord of glory. The people were pierced to the heart, and said, "Men and brethren, what shall we do?" It was an important question, asked for the first time after the apostles received their world-wide Commission. The answer is in these words: "Then Peter said unto them, Repent, and be baptized, every one of you, in the name of Jesus Christ, for the remission of sins, and ye shall receive the gift of the Holy Ghost. For the promise is unto you, and to your children, and to all that are afar off, even as many as the Lord our God shall call" (Acts ii. 38, 39). No one says that the command "Repent" is applicable to infants, and it is certain that the injunction "Be baptized" has no reference to them; for it is as clear as the sun in heaven that the same persons are commanded to repent and be baptized. Then too it ought to be remembered that it would not be rational to address a command to unconscious infants. It is supposed by some, however, that the words "the promise is to you and to your children" refer to infants. The term "children," however, evidently means "posterity;" and the promise cannot be divested of its relation to the Holy Spirit. This promise was not only to the Jews and their posterity, but to Gentiles. The latter are referred to in the words "to all that are afar off." This restriction is laid upon the promise "Even as many as the Lord our God shall call." Whether the word "call" is used in its general sense, as in Prov. viii. 4, "Unto you, O men, I call," or in its special sense, as in 1 Cor. i. 24, "But unto them which are called, both Jews and Greeks," it is in either case inapplicable to infants.

Did any obey Peter's command "Be baptized"? It is written, "Then they that gladly received his word were baptized: and the same day there were added unto them about three thousand souls" (Acts ii. 41). The baptism was limited to those who gladly received Peter's word; and, as infants were not of that number, to infer that they were baptized is utterly gratuitous. There is nothing in the Pentecostal administration of baptism which intimates that infants were considered proper subjects of the ordinance. Let it not be forgotten that the converts on the day of Pentecost were the first persons baptized under the Apostolic Commission, and therefore we have in their baptism the first practical exposition of its true meaning.

There is nothing like infant baptism in the account

given of Philip's labors in Samaria. The reader can examine for himself the eighth chapter of the Acts of the Apostles. There it will be seen that Philip began to execute the Commission by *preaching:* he "preached Christ unto them." He doubtless remembered the words of the risen Redeemer: "Go ye into all the world and preach the gospel to every creature. He that believeth and is baptized shall be saved." The Samaritans "believed Philip preaching the things concerning the kingdom of God and the name of Jesus Christ;" and what then? It is said, "They were baptized, both men and women." Here the Commission of Christ was practically expounded. Is there anything in the exposition which can suggest the idea of "infant dedication to God in baptism"? Surely not. Philip's plan of operation was evidently uniform. Hence, when he fell in with the Ethiopian eunuch—as we learn from the latter part of the same chapter—he first "*preached* unto him Jesus." The eunuch professed *faith* in the Messiah. Then Philip *baptized* him. As "faith comes by hearing, and hearing by the word of God" (Rom. x. 17), there must be preaching before faith, and there must be faith before baptism, because this is the order established by Christ in the Great Commission. Alas for those who invert this order!

SECTION IV.

The argument from household baptisms in favor of infant baptism is invalid.

I will refer to these baptisms as they are recorded in the Scriptures. In the tenth chapter of the Acts of the Apostles there is an account of Peter's visit to Cornelius. He began at Cæsarea to preach to Gentiles as he had before preached to Jews. He carried into effect the Great Commission in precisely the same way. The Holy Spirit accompanied the word preached, and Gentile believers for the first time "spoke with tongues and magnified God." Then said Peter, "Can any man forbid water, that these should not be baptized, who have received the Holy Ghost as well as we? And he commanded them to be baptized in the name of the Lord." Here was a household baptism, but there are things said of the subjects of this baptism that could not be true of speechless infants. One fact, however, settles the whole matter. In the second verse of the chapter it is said that Cornelius "feared God with all his house." Can infants fear God?

The baptism of Lydia and her household at Philippi is next in order. The narrative, as given in Acts xvi. 13, 14, 15, is as follows: "And on the sabbath we went out of the city by a river side, where prayer was wont to be made; and we sat down, and spake unto the women which resorted thither. And a certain woman named Lydia, a seller of purple, of the city of Thyatira, which worshipped God, heard us: whose heart the Lord opened, that she attended unto the things which were spoken of Paul. And when she was baptized, and her household, she besought us, saying, If ye have judged me to be faithful to the Lord, come into my house and abide there. And she constrained us." No one denies that Lydia was a believer; she was therefore a proper subject of baptism. But it is inferred by Pedobaptists that, as her household was baptized, infants must have been baptized. This does not follow, for the very good reason that there are many households in which there are no infants. The probability—and it amounts almost to a certainty—is that Lydia had neither husband nor children. She was engaged in secular business—was "a seller of purple, of the city of Thyatira," which was a considerable distance from Philippi. If she had a husband and infant children, is it not reasonable to suppose that her husband would have taken on himself the business in which she was engaged, letting her remain at home with the infant children? She evidently had no husband with her; for we cannot believe that she violated conjugal propriety so far as to reduce her husband to a cipher by saying "*my house.*" Nor can we believe that the sacred historian would have spoken of "the house of Lydia," in verse 40, if she had a husband. The most reasonable inference is that her household consisted of persons in her employ, that they as well as Lydia became Christian converts, and that they were the "brethren" whom Paul and Silas "comforted" when, having been released from prison, they "entered into the house of Lydia." Enough has been said to invalidate Pedobaptist objections to the Baptist explanation of this narrative, and nothing more can be required. Pedobaptists affirm that Lydia had infant children. Their argument rests for its basis on this view. On them devolves the burden of proof. They must prove that she had infant children. This they have never done—this they can never do. The narrative therefore furnishes no argument in favor of infant baptism.

The same chapter (Acts xvi.) contains an account of the baptism of the jailer and his household. Here it is necessary to say but little; for every one can see that there were no infants in the jailer's family. Paul and Silas "spake unto him the word of the Lord, and to all that were in his house." It is also said that the jailer rejoiced, "believing in God with all his house." Surely the word of the Lord was not spoken to infants; surely infants are incapable of believing. It is worthy of notice that this record shows how Paul understood the Commission of Christ. He first spoke the word of the Lord, and when that word was believed, but not till then, was there an administration of baptism.

It is only necessary to refer to the household of Crispus (Acts xviii. 8) to show what has just been shown—namely, that a man's house as well as himself may believe on the Lord. It is not said in so many words that the family of Crispus was baptized, but it is said that he "believed on the Lord with all his house." No doubt the family was baptized, but faith in Christ preceded the baptism.

In 1 Cor. i. 16, Paul says, "And I baptized also the household of Stephanas." Will any one infer that there were infants in this family? This inference cannot be drawn, in view of what the same apostle says in the same Epistle (xvi. 15): "Ye know the house of Stephanas, that it is the first-fruits of Achaia, and that they have addicted themselves to the ministry of the saints." Infants could not addict themselves to the ministry of the saints. It follows that there were no infants in the family of Stephanas. I am aware that to invalidate this conclusion an argument from chronology has been used. It has been urged that, although infants were baptized in the family of Stephanas when Paul planted the church at Corinth, sufficient time elapsed between their baptism and the date of Paul's First Epistle to the church to justify the declaration, "They have addicted themselves to the ministry of the saints." This argument avails nothing in view of the fact that the most liberal chronology allows only a few years to have intervened between the planting of the church and the date of the Epistle.

Reference has now been made to all the household baptisms mentioned in the New Testament, and there is no proof that there was an infant in any of them. On the other hand, facts and circumstances are related which render it a moral certainty that there were no infants in those baptized families. It will not do to say that ordinarily there are infants in households; it must be shown that it is universally the case. Then the household argument will avail Pedobaptists—not till then. But it cannot be said of all households that there are infants in them. Many a Baptist minister in the United States has baptized more households than are referred to in the New Testament, and no infants in them. It is said that more than thirty entire household baptisms have occurred in connection with American Baptist missionary operations among the Karens in Burmah. In view of such considerations as have now been presented, the reasonings of Pedobaptists from household baptisms are utterly inconclusive. They cannot satisfy a logical mind.

SECTION V.

Certain passages in the New Testament supposed by some Pedobaptists to refer to infant baptism shown to have no such reference.

Conspicuous among these passages is what Paul says in Rom. xi. of the "good olive tree" and of the "wild olive tree." It is assumed that by the "good olive tree" is meant the "Jewish church-state." This assumption requires another—namely, that the "wild olive tree" denotes a Gentile church-state; but from the latter view the most earnest Pedobaptist recoils. The truth is there is no reference by the apostle to any "church-state," whether among Jews or Gentiles. Paul teaches in substance what we learn from other parts of the New Testament—that the Jews enjoyed great privileges, which they abused; in consequence of which abuse, the privileges were taken from them and given to the Gentiles. This is the teaching of Christ; for he said to the Jews, "The kingdom of God shall be taken from you, and given to a nation bringing forth the fruits thereof" (Matt. xxi. 43).

Why this kingdom was taken from the Jews we may learn from John i. 11: "He came unto his own, and his own received him not." They rejected the Messiah who came in fulfilment of their own prophecies, and thus they surrendered the vantage-ground which they had occupied for centuries; and the blessings of the gospel which they refused to accept were offered to, and accepted by, the Gentiles. In this way what Paul elsewhere calls "the blessing of Abraham" was seen to "come on the Gentiles through Jesus Christ" (Gal. iii. 14). The promise of the Spirit was received through faith; for it was by faith that the Gentiles were brought into union with Christ. We see, therefore, the force of Paul's language addressed to a Gentile believer in Rom. xi. 19, 20: "Thou wilt say then, The branches were broken off that I might be graffed in. Well; because of unbelief they were broken off, and thou standest by faith." The reference to faith shows that there is no allusion to infants, who cannot believe. So it appears that the imagery of "the olive tree" affords neither aid nor comfort to the cause of infant baptism.

Pedobaptists appeal with great confidence to 1 Cor. vii. 14 in support of their views. The words are these: "For the unbelieving husband is sanctified by the wife, and the unbelieving wife is sanctified by the husband: else were your children unclean; but now are they holy." It will be seen on examination that there is not in this language the remotest reference to infant baptism. What are the facts in the case? Simply these: The question was agitated at Corinth whether believing husbands and wives should not separate themselves from their unbelieving partners. The idea was entertained—by some, at least—that an unbeliever was "unclean" to a believer, even as, under the Mosaic dispensation, a Gentile was "unclean" to a Jew. Paul corrects this false impression by showing that the unbelieving husband is sanctified—or, rather, has been sanctified—by the wife. The perfect tense is used—a fact ignored by Drs. Conant and Davidson in their revisions, but fully recognized by Dr. Noyes. Without entering into a critical discussion of the word "sanctified," I avail myself of the fact that the sanctification was such as to justify the continuance of the marriage-relation between the believing and the unbelieving partner: "else"—that is, if the sanctification did not remove the supposed "uncleanness" from unbelieving parents—"were your children unclean, but now are they holy." As the verb translated "were" is in the present tense, it should be rendered "are:" "else your children are unclean, but now are they holy." The pronoun "your" deserves special notice. The apostle does not say *their* children—that is, the children of the believing and the unbelieving partner—but *your* children, the children of the parents who were members of the Corinthian church. It follows that the passage under review is intensely strong against infant baptism. It shows that the children of the members of the church sustained the same relation to the church that unbelieving husbands and wives did, and that if believing husbands and wives abandoned their unbelieving partners, then believing parents might, with the same propriety, separate themselves from their children.

Perhaps the exposition of this passage given by a well-known Pedobaptist will be more satisfactory than mine. Rev. Albert Barnes says: "There is not one word about baptism here; not one allusion to it; nor does the argument in the remotest degree bear upon it. The question was not whether children should be baptized, but it was whether there should be a separation between man and wife where the one was a Christian and the other not. Paul states that if such a separation should take place, it would *imply* that the marriage was improper; and *of course* the children must be regarded as unclean." *

Thus it appears that this passage—so often made the basis of Pedobaptist argument—affords no support to the theory or the practice of infant baptism.

SECTION VI.

The allusions to baptism in the Apostolic Epistles forbid the supposition that infants were baptized.

Paul refers to the baptized as "dead to sin," or, rather, as having "died to sin." He asks, "How

* Barnes's *Notes on First Corinthians*, p. 133.

shall we, that are dead to sin [that died to sin], live any longer therein? Know ye not, that so many of us as were baptized into Jesus Christ were baptized into his death?" (Rom. vi. 2, 3). What is meant by dying to sin cannot be exemplified in unconscious infants. In 1 Cor. xv. 29 we have these words: "Else what shall they do which are baptized for the dead, if the dead rise not at all? why are they then baptized for the dead?" The controverted phrase "baptized for the dead," occurring, as it does, in the midst of an argument on the resurrection, most probably means "baptized in the belief of the resurrection." Such a belief cannot be predicated of infants. In Gal. iii. 27 it is written, "For as many of you as have been baptized into Christ have put on Christ." These words cannot apply to infants, because they are incapable of putting on Christ. In Col. ii. 12 the record is, "Buried with him in baptism, wherein also ye are risen with him through the faith of the operation of God, who hath raised him from the dead." However true and consoling may be the doctrine of infant salvation, it is not true that infants are risen with Christ "through the faith of the operation of God." If, in 1 Tim. vi. 12, the language, "hast professed a good profession before many witnesses," refers to the baptismal profession, it is evident that such a profession cannot be made by those in a state of infancy. Dr. Davidson translates "didst confess the good confession before many witnesses," which is strictly literal, for the Greek verb refers to past time. In Heb. x. 22 we find the expression "our bodies washed with pure water." If there is in these words an allusion to baptism (and I think there is), it is plain that the same persons who were baptized had been set free from "an evil conscience." No infant has "an evil conscience."

Peter, in his First Epistle (iii. 21), defines baptism to be "the answer of a good conscience toward God by the resurrection of Jesus Christ." This is a general definition, and it forbids the idea that baptism, in apostolic times, was administered to any but accountable agents. What conscience has an infant? There is no operation of conscience before accountability. Baptism, then, in its administration to infants, cannot be what Peter says it is. This is for Pedobaptists an unfortunate fact—a fact which shows their practice to be unscriptural.

There is in this connection another thing worthy of consideration. Paul, in his Epistles to the Ephesians and Colossians, exhorts children to obey their parents. It is generally supposed that about five years intervened between the introduction of the gospel into Ephesus and Colosse and the writing of Paul's Epistles. Now, if those children, or any of them, had been baptized when the gospel was introduced into these cities, is it not strange that the apostle, in urging upon them obedience, presented no motive derived from their dedication to God in baptism? There is no allusion to any "vows, promises, and obligations" made and assumed for them by their parents or sponsors at their baptism. There is nothing said that bears a resemblance to a personal acceptance of a draft drawn upon them in anticipation of their intelligence and responsibility. Here a query may be presented: Would a Pedobaptist apostle have pursued this course? To bring the matter nearer home: Would a Pedobaptist missionary write a letter to a Pedobaptist church, making special mention of parents and children, urging both to a faithful performance of relative duties, and say nothing about the obligations of either parents or children as connected with infant baptism or growing out of it? No one will answer this question affirmatively. The apostle of the Gentiles, therefore, did what we cannot reasonably imagine a Pedobaptist missionary or minister to do. This is a very suggestive fact.

I have now noticed the usual arguments supposed to be furnished by the New Testament in favor of infant baptism. Not one has been intentionally omitted. Is there precept or example to justify it? Celebrated Pedobaptist authors shall answer this question. Dr.

Wall of the Church of England, in his *History of Infant Baptism,* on the very first page of his "Preface," says that, "among all the persons that are recorded as baptized by the apostles, there is no express mention of any infant." Neander of Germany—the first church historian of his generation—referring to "the latter part of the apostolic age," expresses himself thus: "As baptism was closely united with a conscious entrance on Christian communion, faith and baptism were always connected with one another; and thus it is in the highest degree probable that baptism was performed only in instances where both could meet together, and that the practice of infant baptism was unknown at this period. We cannot infer the existence of infant baptism from the instance of the baptism of whole families, for the passage in 1 Cor. xvi. 15 shows the fallacy of such a conclusion, as from that it appears that the whole family of Stephanas, who were baptized by Paul, consisted of adults."* Professor Moses Stuart, for many years the glory of the Andover Theological Seminary, in his *Essay on Baptism* (p. 101), says, in his reference to infant baptism, "Commands or plain and certain examples, in the New Testament, relative to it, I do not find. Nor, with my views of it, do I need them." Dr. Woods, long a colleague of Professor Stuart, in his *Lectures on*

* *Planting and Training of the Church,* pp. 101, 102.

Infant Baptism, remarks as follows: "It is a plain case that there is no express precept respecting infant baptism in our sacred writings. The proof, then, that infant baptism is a divine institution must be made out in another way." These are important concessions, made by men whose celebrity is coextensive with Christendom.

Now, if the New Testament does not sustain the cause of infant baptism, ought it not to be given up? If, as the Westminster Confession affirms, "baptism is a sacrament of the New Testament, ordained by Jesus Christ," it is self-evident that we should go to the New Testament to learn who are proper subjects of baptism. If it was ordained by Jesus Christ, we should allow him to decide who are to be baptized, and not refer the matter to either Abraham or Moses. But Pedobaptists, unable to prove infant baptism from the New Testament, go to the Old, and try to sustain it by reasoning, analogy, inference. Was there ever before such a course adopted to establish a divine ordinance? Ask a Jew why his ancestors for so many centuries observed the feasts of the Passover, Pentecost, and Tabernacles, and he will tell you that God commanded them to do so. Ask a Christian why believers should be baptized and partake of the Lord's Supper, and his response will be that these are injunctions of Jesus Christ. Ask a Pedobaptist, however, why infants should be baptized, and he will at once plunge into the mazes of Judaism and argue the identity of the old "Jewish Church" and the gospel church, insisting, meanwhile, on the substitution of baptism for circumcision. This is a strange method of proving that infants ought to be baptized. It argues a consciousness of the utter absence of New-Testament authority for infant baptism. It indicates that there is no command to baptize infants; for a command would supersede the necessity of *argument* to show the propriety of the practice. No man enters into an argument to prove that believers should be baptized. The positive injunction of Christ renders it superfluous. Strange as it is for Pedobaptists to go to the Old Testament for justification of one of their practices under the New-Testament economy, yet, as they do so, it is necessary to follow them. This will now be done.

SECTION VII.

The argument from the supposed identity of the Jewish commonwealth and the gospel church of no force.

This identity is assumed, and on it the propriety of infant church-membership is thought to rest. I shall permit distinguished Pedobaptist writers—representative men—to speak for themselves. Dr. Hibbard, a very able Methodist author, in his work on *Christian Baptism*, says: "Our next proper position relates to the substantial oneness or identity of the Jewish and Christian churches. I say *substantial* oneness, because, although in many secondary and adventitious points they differ, still, in all the essential features of the real church of God, they are one and the same. And here it is proper to admonish the reader of the importance of this position. It is upon this ground that we rest the weight of the Bible argument for infant baptism" (pp. 31, 32).

This language is plain and easily understood, though any one familiar with the baptismal controversy will detect in the phrase "*substantial* oneness" an unwillingness to endorse the "identity" theory without qualification.

Dr. Samuel Miller, for many years Professor of Ecclesiastical History in Princeton Theological Seminary, in his *Sermons on Baptism,* expresses himself thus: "As the infant seed of the people of God are acknowledged on all hands to have been members of the church equally with their parents under the Old-Testament Dispensation, *so it is equally certain that the church of God is the same in substance now that it was then."* The *italics* are the Doctor's. Here, also, is a disposition to recoil from a bold avowal of the doctrine of identity. "*The same in substance"* is the convenient phrase selected to meet the logical exigences that may possibly occur. Again, Dr. Miller says: "It is not more certain that a man arrived at mature age is the same individual that he was when an infant on his mother's lap, than it is that the church, in the plentitude of her light and privileges after the coming of Christ, is the same church which many centuries before, though with a much smaller amount of light and privilege, yet, as we are expressly told in the New Testament (Acts vii. 38), enjoyed the presence and guidance of her Divine Head in the wilderness." *

Dr. N. L. Rice, in his debate with the renowned Alexander Campbell at Lexington, Kentucky, remarks, "*The church, then, is the same under the Jewish and Christian Dispensations—the same into which God did, by positive law, put believers and their children.*" † Dr. Rice, it will be seen, is bolder than Drs. Hibbard and Miller. He says nothing about "substantial oneness," "the same in substance;" but with characteristic fearlessness announces his position, and, in order to attract special attention, *italicizes* the words in which he expresses it.

The venerable Dr. Charles Hodge, in his *Theology*, is as positive in his statements as is Dr. Rice. This will be seen in the following extracts: "The commonwealth of Israel was the church. It is so called in Scripture (Acts vii. 38);" "The church under the New Dispensation is identical with that under the

* *Sermons on Baptism*, pp. 18, 19. † *Debate*, p. 285.

Old. It is not a new church, but one and the same;" "Under the old economy, the church and state were identical. No man could be a member of the one without being a member of the other. Exclusion from the one was exclusion from the other. In the pure theocracy the high priest was the head of the state as well as the head of the church. The priests and Levites were civil as well as religious officers" (vol. iii., pp. 548, 549, 552, 553).

As Dr. Hodge held these views, the thoughtful reader will wonder that he was not an advocate of a union between church and state under the gospel economy. That he was not resulted from a fortunate inconsistency on his part.

The Pedobaptist view of the identity of the Jewish theocracy and the Christian Church is now before us as given by men of high position and distinction. Can this view be sustained? I shall attempt to show that it is utterly untenable. First, however, the term *church* must be defined. It means "a congregation," "an assembly." The Greeks used the term *ekklesia* (the word translated "church") to signify an assembly, without regard to the purpose for which the assembly met. Hence the tumultuous concourse of the citizens of Ephesus referred to in Acts xix. 32, 41, is called in the original *ekklesia,* and is translated "assembly." We have the same word in verse 39; but, as a defining epithet is prefixed to it, we read in the common version "lawful assembly." The term *ekklesia*, therefore, while it denotes an assembly, does not, in its general signification, denote the *kind* of assembly. This being the case, the Jewish nation, or congregation, might with propriety be called *ekklesia*, or "church," as in Acts vii. 38. In the New Testament, however, the term *ekklesia*, in its application to the followers of Christ, generally refers to a particular local congregation of saints. I do not say that it has not a more extensive meaning, but this is its general meaning; and with this alone the present argument is concerned. The sacred writers speak of the *churches* of Judea, the *churches* of Macedonia, the *churches* of Asia, the *churches* of Galatia; and these churches were evidently composed of persons who had made credible profession of their faith in Christ. In apostolic times the members of a particular congregation were called "saints," "believers," "disciples," "brethren." They were separated from the world—a spiritual people. Baptists say that in this sense of the term "church" there was no church before the Christian Dispensation. There were doubtless many pious persons from the days of Abel to the coming of Christ, but there was not a body of saints separate from the world. The Jewish nation was separate from other nations, but it was not a nation of saints. It was a kind of politico-religious body, and circumcision was a mark of nationality. The righteous and the wicked belonged to this commonwealth and were entitled to its privileges. But there was no spiritual organization composed of regenerate persons, called out, separated, from the Jews as a people, till John the Baptist came preaching in the wilderness of Judea. I have been thus particular in defining the term "church" that there may be no misapprehension of its meaning. Where the phrase "Jewish Church" is used it is to be understood as denoting—as in Acts vii. 38—the whole nation, and not a true spiritual body. But where the phrase "Christian Church" occurs it denotes a body of regenerate, spiritual believers in Christ.

I now proceed to show that the Jewish theocracy and the kingdom of God, or of heaven, as referred to in the New Testament, are not identical.

1. *Because, when the Jewish theocracy had been in existence for centuries, the prophets predicted the establishment of a new kingdom.*

In Isaiah ii. 2 it is written, "And it shall come to pass in the last days, that the mountain of the Lord's house shall be established in the top of the mountains, and shall be exalted above the hills; and all nations shall flow unto it." There is manifest reference here to the kingdom of God. It is not intimated that this kingdom had been established, but that it was to be es-

DISTINCTIVE PRINCIPLES OF BAPTISTS. 45

tablished. The phrase "last days" means, no doubt, what it means in Heb. i. 1, 2: "God . . . hath in these last days spoken unto us by his Son." It designates the period of the Christian Dispensation.

The prophecy of Daniel (ii. 44) deserves special consideration. Having referred, in the interpretation of Nebuchadnezzar's dream, to the empires of Babylon, Medo-Persia, Greece, and Rome, the prophet added, "And in the days of these kings shall the God of heaven set up a kingdom, which shall never be destroyed; and the kingdom shall not be left to other people, but it shall break in pieces and consume all these kingdoms, and it shall stand for ever." This kingdom was to be set up several centuries after Daniel prophesied. The phrase "set up" must indicate the establishment of a new kingdom; there is no intimation that the old Jewish kingdom was to be reorganized. This new kingdom was to stand for ever. It was not to fall, like the worldly empires symbolized by the gold, silver, brass, and iron of Nebuchadnezzar's image, but it was to be a permanent kingdom, maintaining an unbroken existence amid the lapse of ages and the revolutions of time. Who does not see that this kingdom has an inseparable connection with the church of Christ, of which he said, "The gates of hell shall not prevail against it"? (Matt. xvi. 18). The kingdom, the church, is to stand.

Why? Because the machinations of Satan cannot overthrow it.

John the Baptist referred in his preaching to the *new* kingdom. His voice was heard in the wilderness of Judea, saying, "Repent ye; for the kingdom of heaven is at hand" (Matt. iii. 2). Was it the old Jewish kingdom that was at hand? Certainly not. Jesus too, in the very beginning of his ministry, announced the same kingdom as "at hand." He said, "The time is fulfilled, and the kingdom of God is at hand: repent ye, and believe the gospel" (Mark i. 15). The time to which the prophets, Daniel especially, referred was fulfilled. The new kingdom was at hand. The command, therefore, was "Repent ye." Such preaching had never before been heard. The injunction "Repent" was new, and the argument enforcing it was new. There was something so novel and so distinctive in the preaching of Christ and his harbinger as to indicate the introduction of a new era. That the preaching of John was the beginning of a new era is manifest from the Saviour's words: "The law and the prophets were until John: since that time the kingdom of God is preached, and every man presseth into it" (Luke xvi. 16).

In view of the considerations now presented, how can the Jewish theocracy and the gospel kingdom be the same? Is "the substantial oneness, or identity, of the Jewish and Christian churches"—to use Dr. Hibbard's words—a possible thing? Yet he says, "It is upon this ground that we rest the weight of the Bible argument for infant baptism." It rests, then, on a foundation of sand. Dr. Hibbard is in a dilemma. He may choose either horn of this dilemma, and it will gore him unmercifully. For if such a foundation can sustain the argument for infant baptism, there is no *weight* in the argument; but if the weight of the argument crushes the foundation, there is no *solidity* in the foundation.

2. *Another fact fatal to the identity contended for is that those who were regular members of the old Jewish Church could not become members of the Christian Church without repentance, faith, regeneration, and baptism.*

The plainness of this proposition renders it needless to dwell upon it at any great length. A few considerations will sufficiently develop its truth. The inhabitants of Judea were, of course, members of the "Jewish Church." I prefer the phrase "Jewish commonwealth" or "Jewish theocracy," because in our ordinary language the word "church" carries with it the Christian idea of a truly spiritual body; but through courtesy I say "Jewish Church," as explained above.

The Jews in Jerusalem and in the land of Judea were members of this church. John the Baptist called on these church-members to repent and do works meet for repentance and to believe on the coming Messiah as preparatory to baptism. He restricted the administration of baptism to those who repented and believed. The Pharisees and Sadducees—two prominent sects among the Jews—were church-members. John spoke to them as a "generation of vipers." The Pharisees had no adequate conception of the necessity of a proper state of heart, and the Sadducees were semi-infidels. They were no doubt recognized as worthy members of the Jewish Church, but they were utterly unfit for membership in a church of Christ. John let them know that their relationship to Abraham was no qualification for a place in the kingdom of heaven. Nicodemus was a Pharisee and an *official* member of this Jewish Church; yet he was ignorant of the doctrine of regeneration. Being "born again" was a mystery to him. He was an unregenerate man. The Saviour said to him, "Marvel not that I said unto thee, Ye must be born again" (John iii. 7). Nor did Jesus regard any of the Jews as qualified for baptism till they became his disciples. It is therefore said that he "made and baptized more disciples than John" (John iv. 1). The scribes, lawyers, and doctors of the Jewish Church the Great Teacher denounced as hypocrites; "for," he said, "ye shut up the kingdom of heaven against men: for ye neither go in yourselves, neither suffer ye them that are entering to go in"

(Matt. xxiii. 13). This passage proves two things—that the kingdom of heaven was then in existence, and that it was not identical with the Jewish kingdom. If it had not been in existence, it could not have been shut up. If it was identical with the Jewish kingdom, the scribes were already in it. But they were not in it; for the Saviour said, "Ye neither go in yourselves." If, then, they were in the Jewish kingdom, and were not in the kingdom of heaven, the two kingdoms cannot be the same.

3. *It deserves special notice that the covenant of the Jewish Church and the covenant of the Christian Church are different.*

The truth of this proposition Pedobaptists deny. They assume that "the covenant of grace," or "gospel covenant," was made with Abraham, and that the "covenant of circumcision" was so identified with it that circumcision became the seal of "the covenant of grace."

Dr. Thomas O. Summers, now (1882) Professor of Theology in Vanderbilt University, in his volume on *Baptism* (p. 23), referring to infants, says: "They are specifically embraced in the gospel covenant. When that covenant was made with Abraham, his children were brought under its provisions, and the same seal that was administered to him was administered also to them, including both those that were born in his house and those that were bought with his money. They were all alike circumcised in token of their common interest in that covenant of which circumcision was the appointed symbol. That covenant is still in force."

Dr. Hodge, as already quoted, not only says that "the church under the New Dispensation is identical with that under the Old," but adds, "It is founded on the same covenant—the covenant made with Abraham." Again he says: "Such being the nature of the covenant made with Abraham, it is plain that, so far as its main element is concerned, it is still in force. It is the covenant of grace, under which we now live, and upon which the church is now founded" (vol. iii., pp. 549, 550).

Here it is assumed by these two able writers, who worthily represent Methodists and Presbyterians, that the gospel covenant was *made* with Abraham, and that circumcision was its seal. Pedobaptists have a decided preference for the singular number. They do not say *covenants:* it is *covenant* in conversation, in books, and in sermons. Paul speaks of *covenants*, the two *covenants*, *covenants* of promise, etc. How "the covenant of circumcision" can be identified with "the covenant of grace," or "gospel covenant," defies ordinary comprehension. Placing myself in antagonism with Drs. Summers and Hodge, I am obliged to say that what the former calls the "gospel covenant," and the latter "the covenant of grace," was not *made* with Abraham. They both quote Paul, but Paul does not say so. The language of the apostle is this: "And this I say, That the covenant that was confirmed before of God in Christ [that is, in reference to the Messiah] the law, which was four hundred and thirty years after, cannot disannul, that it should make the promise of none effect" (Gal. iii. 17). This covenant was *confirmed* to Abraham, not *made* with him. It was made before. It must have had an existence, or it could not have been confirmed. The confirmation of anything implies its previous existence.

I shall not attempt to penetrate the counsels of eternity to ascertain the particulars of the origin of the covenant of grace. It is sufficient for my present purpose to say that it is, doubtless, the result of the sublime consultation of the three Persons in the Godhead concerning the prospective condemnation and ruin of the race of Adam. The first intimation of the existence of this covenant was given in the memorable words, "And I will put enmity between thee and the woman, and between thy seed and her seed: it shall bruise thy head, and thou shalt bruise his heel" (Gen. iii. 15). This incipient development of God's purpose of mercy to man no doubt cheered Abel, Enoch, and all the pious who lived in the world's infancy. The nature of the covenant, recognized when mercy's faint whisperings were first heard, was more fully unfolded when that covenant was *confirmed* to Abraham in the words, "And in thee shall all families of the earth be blessed;" "And in thy seed shall all the nations of the earth be blessed" (Gen. xii. 3; xxii. 18). These two promises are substantially the same, the one affirming that in Abraham, the other that in his seed, all the families, or nations, of the earth should be blessed. There was to be no blessing from him personally to all nations, but the blessing was to come through his seed. Irrespective of the provisions of the covenant confirmed to Abraham, there never has been, and never will be, salvation for Jew or Gentile. There is no salvation except in Christ, and Paul informs us that he is referred to as the "seed" of Abraham: "He saith not, And to seeds, as of many; but as of one, And to thy seed, which is Christ" (Gal. iii. 16). The covenant with respect to Christ, if we count from the first promise to Abraham, was *confirmed* to him when seventy-five years old (Gen. xii.), and the covenant of circumcision was *made* with him when he had reached his ninety-ninth year (Gen. xvii.). Twenty-four years intervened between the two transactions, yet Pedobaptists insist that there was but one covenant. One covenant was *confirmed* to Abraham, and one *made* with him; yet, it seems, there was but one! There is some mistake about this, for two *ones* added together make *two*.

Now, if, according to the theory of Drs. Summers and Hodge, the "gospel covenant," or "covenant of grace," was made with Abraham, and if circumcision was the seal of that covenant, then it had no seal for twenty-four years after it was made. Moreover, if the "gospel covenant," or "covenant of grace," was *made* with Abraham, by the provisions of what covenant were Abel, Enoch, Noah, and others who lived before the days of Abraham, saved? This question is submitted to all the Pedobaptist theologians in Christendom. If they will only consider it, they will cease to say that the "gospel covenant," or "covenant of grace," was *made* with Abraham. If, as Pedobaptists assert, circumcision was the seal of the "covenant of grace," what became of Abraham's female descendants? Were the blessings of the covenant not secured to them, or were they left to the "uncovenanted mercies" of God? The truth is the inspired writers never refer to circumcision or baptism as a "seal" of a covenant. Circumcision is called "a token of the covenant" which God made with Abraham (Gen. xvii. 11), and "a seal of the righteousness of the faith which he had, yet being uncircumcised" (Rom. iv. 11). It was never a seal of the righteousness of the faith of any other man. How could it be, when all Abraham's male descendants were required to be circumcised at eight days old, when they were incapable of faith? Under the Gospel Dispensation baptism is not a seal, and Pedobaptists labor under a mistake when they so represent it. Believers are "sealed with that Holy Spirit of promise" (Eph. i. 13). They are commanded to "grieve not the Holy Spirit of God whereby ye are sealed unto the day of redemption" (Eph. iv. 30). But, for argument's sake, let baptism be considered a seal—a seal of the covenant which, it is said, was formerly sealed by circumcision. Then the perplexing question arises, Why apply the seal to both sexes, when the seal of circumcision was applied to but one? Circumcision, it is argued, was a type of baptism. The type had reference to males alone. Therefore the antitype has reference to both sexes! Such reasoning is at war with the plainest principles of sound logic. There is another absurdity in making baptism the antitype of circumcision. Baptism is referred to by Peter as a "figure." If, then, circumcision was a type of it, it was a type of a type, a figure of a figure; which is incredible.

But to be more specific with regard to the covenants: The covenant of circumcision made with Abraham received its full development in the covenant of Mount Sinai. There was, if the expression is allowable, a new edition of the covenant. The Sinaitic regulations were made in pursuance of the provisions of the covenant made with Abraham, and on this account circumcision, the "token of the covenant," was incorporated into those regulations, and became a rite of the Mosaic economy. Jesus therefore said to the Jews, "If a man on the sabbath day receive circumcision that the law of Moses should not be broken," etc. (John vii. 23). This language shows that the covenant of circumcision was so identified with the Sinaitic covenant that the failure to circumcise a man was a violation of the law of Moses. The old Jewish Church, then, grew out of the covenant of circumcision, which was the germ of the Sinaitic covenant that God made with the Israelites when he "took them by the hand to lead them out of the land of Egypt" (Heb. viii. 9). This covenant, entered into at Mount Sinai, was to continue in force, and did continue in force, till superseded by another and a "better covenant." It preserved the nationality of the Jews, while circumcision marked that nationality and indicated a *natural* relationship to Abraham. This celebrated patriarch was to have a numerous *natural* seed, to which reference is made in the covenant of circumcision, and, by virtue of the provisions of the covenant "*confirmed*" to him concerning the Messiah, he was to have a *spiritual* seed also. He was to be the father of believers. Hence we have such passages of Scripture as these: "That he might be the father of all them that believe, though they be not circumcised" (Rom. iv. 2); "They which are of faith, the same are the children of Abraham;" "And if ye be Christ's, then are ye Abraham's seed, and heirs according to the promise" (Gal. iii. 7, 29). The process of *spiritual filiation* to Abraham is effected by faith. Jews, therefore—his natural seed—cannot become his spiritual seed without faith. But if faith creates the *spiritual* relationship to Abraham, Gentiles as well as Jews may become his spiritual seed, for they are equally capable of faith. For the encouragement of Gentiles who were uncircumcised, Paul referred to the fact that Abraham was justified by faith *before* he was circumcised. Having referred to the development of the Abrahamic covenant of circumcision in the covenant of Sinai, I may now refer to the development of the covenant respecting the Messiah, out of which covenant has grown the gospel church. This is termed the *new* covenant, in contradistinction from the Sinaitic covenant. The development of its provisions was to occur many centuries subsequent to the giving of the law, although those provisions had an embryo existence in the covenant "confirmed" to Abraham concerning Christ. In Heb. viii. 8–12 there is a quotation from Jer. xxxi. 31–34 which sheds much light on the two covenants. It is as follows: "Behold the days come, saith the Lord, when I will make a new covenant with the house of Israel and with the house of Judah: not according to the covenant that I made with their fathers, in the day when I took them by the hand to lead them out of the land of Egypt; because they continued not in my covenant, and I regarded them not, saith the Lord. For this is the covenant that I will make with the house of Israel after those days, saith the Lord; I will put my laws into their mind, and write them in their hearts: and I will be to them a God, and they shall be to me a people: and they shall not teach every man his neighbor, and every man his brother, saying, Know the Lord: for all shall know me from the least to the greatest. For I will be merciful to their unrighteousness, and their sins and their iniquities will I remember no more."

This is the new covenant—*new* in its manifestation, though *old* in its origin—the "better covenant, which was established upon better promises" (Heb. viii. 6). Of this covenant Jesus is Mediator, and this fact shows that the gospel covenant is the outgrowth of the covenant "confirmed of God" to Abraham concerning Christ. How essentially different the old covenant and the new! Pedobaptists, however, as we have seen, insist that the Jewish Church and the Christian Church are the same! God found fault with the old covenant, and superseded it by the new; yet it seems that the new which displaces the old is substantially identical with it! It is strange that men do not observe that God, in describing the new covenant, says expressly, "NOT ACCORDING TO THE COVENANT THAT I MADE WITH THEIR FATHERS," the old covenant.

Several distinctive points of difference between the old covenant and the new may be seen in Gal. iv. 22–31. There are four allegorical personages referred to by Paul—namely, Hagar, Ishmael, Sarah, and Isaac. Hagar was a "bondmaid," and gave birth to a son "after the flesh"—that is, there was in his birth no departure from the laws of ordinary generation. This "bondwoman" represents the covenant of Sinai, and "answereth to Jerusalem, which now is"—the old Jewish Church, which "gendereth to bondage." Jerusalem—the Jewish Church—is therefore said to be "in bondage with her children." To "gender to bondage" was all that Sinai could do; there was no provision in the Sinaitic covenant for anything more: its possibilities were exhausted. Sarah, "the free woman," represents the new covenant, and the Christian Church of which that covenant is the charter. She gave birth to Isaac, who was born "by promise'—"after the Spirit"—that is, according to a promise the fulfilment of which involved supernatural agency. "Jerusalem which is above"—the Christian Church represented by Sarah—"is free, which is the mother of us all," of all Christians. Believers in Christ are "the children of promise," as Isaac was. They are born "after the Spirit" and "of the Spirit." Thus it is as clear as the light of day that, while the Jewish Church was supplied with its members by *generation*, the Christian Church is furnished with its members by *regeneration*. This is one prominent difference between the two, and it is as great as that between death and immortality. "But as then," says the apostle, "he that was born after the flesh persecuted him that was born after the Spirit, even so it is now." Ishmael persecuted Isaac, and so the children of the covenant of Sinai—Abraham's seed according to the flesh—persecuted, in apostolic times, the beneficiaries of the new covenant, Abraham's spiritual seed. Sinai, in "gendering to bondage," also "gendered" a persecuting spirit; and it is worthy of remark that an infusion of Judaism into the sentiments of any religious denomination has a tendency to make it a persecuting denomination. This fact is both significant and suggestive. "Nevertheless, what saith the scripture? Cast out the bondwoman and her son; for the son of the bondwoman shall not be heir with the son of the free woman. So then, brethren, we are not children of the bondwoman, but of the free."

Here is authority for keeping all but regenerate

persons out of the Christian Church: "Cast out the bondwoman and her son." The Jews, considered as Abraham's natural seed, had no right to the privileges of the church of Christ. They had first to become Christ's disciples by faith, and then they were in the important sense Abraham's seed. Paul never forgot one of the first principles of the gospel economy announced by John the Baptist to the Pharisees and the Sadducees: "Think not to say within yourselves, We have Abraham to our father; for I say unto you, that God is able of these stones to raise up children unto Abraham" (Matt. iii. 9). They were, under the New Dispensation, to claim nothing on the ground of their lineal descent from Abraham. Piety was to be an intensely personal concern. Daniel Webster once said, "The bed of death brings every human being to his pure individuality." This is true; but Christianity does the same thing before it is done by "the bed of death." The gospel places every one on the basis of his "pure individuality" before God.

4. *The supposed identity of the Jewish Church and the Christian Church involves absurdities and impossibilities.*

According to this view, the scribes, the Pharisees, the Sadducees, and all the Jews were members of the church; yet it is notorious that they procured the crucifixion of the Head of the church. These church-members, many of them occupying "official positions," manifested bitter enmity to Christ, and said, "We will not have this man to reign over us." They charged him with being in league with Satan in casting out demons. When he was condemned to death they said, "His blood be on us and on our children" (Matt. xxvii. 25). Strange language for church-members to employ! Who can believe that they were members of a church "the same in substance" with the Christian Church? If the Pedobaptist position is tenable, the three thousand converts on the day of Pentecost were added to the church, though they were in it before! The Lord added daily to the church not only the saved (Acts ii. 47), but those already members! When a great company of priests became obedient to the faith, they joined themselves to the apostles and were put out of the synagogues, though the Jews putting them out were of the same church! Saul of Tarsus "persecuted the church and wasted it" —"made havoc" of it—and when converted became a member of the church, though he had always been one! Ay, more, he obtained his authority to persecute from official members of the church. These and many other absurdities and impossibilities are involved in the supposition that the Jewish Church and the Christian Church are the same. They are not the same. The phrases "same in substance," "substantial identity," cannot avail Pedobaptists; for there is no sort of identity. A "substantial sameness" cannot be discovered with a theological microscope. Paul's teaching is that Jesus Christ makes "of twain one new man" (Eph. ii. 15)—that is, regenerated Jews and Gentiles are the materials of which the new man, or church, is composed. There is reference to an organization, and the descriptive epithet "*new*" is applied to it. Pedobaptists virtually say that the Lord Jesus did not make a "new man." They advocate the claims of the "old man," admitting, however, that he is changed in some unimportant respect; so that his "substantial identity" remains unimpaired.

What effect would have been produced in apostolic times on the minds of unbelieving Jews if it had been intimated that their church was identical with the Christian Church? They would have been highly offended. Paul exemplified the most indignant eloquence whenever false teachers attempted to corrupt the purity of the Christian Church with the leaven of Judaism. The old Jewish Church and the church of the New Testament were regarded by believers and by unbelievers as essentially distinct. No one thought of their "substantial identity;" for infant baptism was unknown, and there was nothing to suggest the "identity" doctrine. It is as easy for a camel to go through the eye of a needle as for the identity of the Jewish and the Christian churches to be maintained. If there is no identity, infant membership in the Jewish commonwealth is no authority for infant membership in the Christian Church; and it is perfectly gratuitous to insist that baptism has come in the place of circumcision. Still, the advocates of infant baptism argue that circumcision is superseded by baptism, and that, as infants were circumcised under the Jewish economy, they should be baptized under the Christian Dispensation.

SECTION VIII.

The argument from circumcision fails.

The position advocated by Pedobaptists will be seen from the following extracts.

Dr. Miller—already referred to—says: " Our next step is to show *that baptism has come in the room of circumcision,* and therefore that the former is rightfully and properly applied to the same subjects as the latter." Again: " There is the best foundation for asserting that baptism has come in the place of circumcision . . . Yet, though baptism manifestly comes in the place of circumcision, there are points in regard to which the former differs materially from the latter." * Here the doctrine is stated unequivocally that " baptism has come in the place of circumcision." How it takes its place, and yet " differs materially from it "

* *Sermons on Baptism,* pp. 22, 23.

on some "points," must ever be a mystery to persons of ordinary mental penetration.

Dr. Rice says: "It is certain that baptism came in place of circumcision; that it answers the same ends in the church now that were answered by circumcision under the former dispensation." *

Dr. Summers affirms: "That baptism is the ordinance of initiation into the church, and the sign and seal of the covenant now, as circumcision was formerly, is evident." †

I find in Dr. Hodge's *Theology* no statements so positive as those now quoted, but he so expresses himself that it is impossible not to infer his belief in the substitution of baptism for circumcision.

But is this view, though held by great and learned men, defensible? I shall attempt to show that it is not, for the following reasons:

1. *It was necessary for the circumcised to be baptized before they could become members of the church of Christ.*

How was this, if baptism came in the place of circumcision and is a seal of the same covenant? Was the covenant first sealed by circumcision, and subsequently sealed by baptism? Were there two seals? If so, away goes the substitution theory. If the same persons were both circumcised and baptized, there was,

---

* *Debate with Campbell,* p. 302.
† *Summers on Baptism,* pp. 25, 26.

DISTINCTIVE PRINCIPLES OF BAPTISTS. 65

so far as they were concerned, no substitution of baptism for circumcision. In their case circumcision was not abolished, and nothing could take its place. It occupied its own place, and it was necessary for that place to be *vacated* before anything else could occupy it. Dr. Miller refers to baptism as coming "*in the room*" of circumcision; but there was no "*room*" till the non-observance of circumcision made room. Why, then, were those who had been circumcised baptized? Why was Jesus himself both circumcised and baptized? These are unanswerable questions if baptism came in the place of circumcision.

Dr. Miller's views involve another difficulty. He says: "The children of professing Christians are already in the church. They were born members; their baptism did not make them members. It was a public ratification and recognition of their membership. They were baptized because they were members" (p. 74). The position here assumed is demolished by one fact. That fact is that the New-Testament subjects of baptism are never represented as baptized because they are in the church, but that they may enter into it. Dr. Miller's reason for administering baptism to infants labors under the misfortune of being remarkably unscriptural; for if "the children of professing Christians are already in the church," this is a very good reason for not baptizing them at all.

Any one familiar with the baptismal controversy can see that Dr. Miller's *Abrahamic* and *Judaistic* notions vitiated his logic in its application to evangelical subjects. He reasoned in this way: The natural seed of Abraham were members of the Jewish National Church by virtue of their birth; and so far his reasoning was correct. They were circumcised because by natural generation they were made beneficiaries of the covenant of which circumcision was the " token." Dr. Miller's next step was this: The children of professing Christians are born members of the Christian Church, and are entitled to baptism, even as Abraham's natural seed were entitled to circumcision. But is this true? It cannot be. Whatever rational analogy may be traced between circumcision and baptism is on the side of the opponents of infant baptism. How plain this is! Abraham's *natural* seed were circumcised because they had a birthright-interest in the covenant God made with Abraham. Christians are Abraham's *spiritual* seed. They become so by faith in Christ, and are beneficiaries of the new covenant, the provisions of which are eminently spiritual. There is in baptism a recognition of their interest in the blessings of this covenant. It was right to circumcise Abraham's natural seed, and it is right to baptize his spiritual seed; but who are his spiritual seed? Believers in Christ, and believers alone. Infants, therefore, have no right to baptism, because they are not Abraham's spiritual seed. Jewish infants were fit subjects for circumcision, because they were Abraham's *natural* seed; but neither Jewish nor Gentile infants can be his *spiritual* seed, because of their incapacity to believe, and therefore they ought not to be baptized. I insist, then, that correct analogical reasoning from circumcision to baptism saps the very foundation of Pedobaptism and furnishes Baptists with an argument of the strength of which they have never fully availed themselves. This may be considered a digression. If so, let us return to the subject of discussion.

I was attempting to show that baptism did not come in the place of circumcision, and referred to the well-known fact that multitudes of circumcised persons were also baptized. This could never have taken place if baptism came in the room of circumcision. In this connection, the circumcision of Timothy is worthy of notice. His mother was a Jewess, but his father a Greek. Owing to the latter fact, doubtless, he remained uncircumcised. After his conversion and baptism Timothy was circumcised by Paul. This was done to conciliate the Jews, which shows that they considered circumcision a mark of nationality. Now the question arises, Why did Paul circumcise Timothy, who had been baptized, if baptism came in the place of circumcision? Thus in the New Testament we have baptism administered after circumcision, and circumcision performed after baptism: yet Pedobaptists say that the one came in the place of the other!

2. *A second fact to be noticed is that circumcision was confined to one sex.*

Premises and conclusions are often wide as the poles asunder. Of this we have a striking proof in the reasoning of Pedobaptists from the circumcision of infants under the Old Dispensation to the baptism of infants under the New. The fact they begin with is of course this: Male children were circumcised under the Old-Testament economy. The conclusion is: Therefore male and female children ought to be baptized under the gospel economy. Is this logic? If but one sex is recognized in the premise, how is it that there is a recognition of both sexes in the conclusion? There must be something wrong in the reasoning that brings out more in conclusions than is contained in premises. This is the misfortune of the argument now under consideration. Pedobaptists most gratuitously infer that, as children of one sex were formerly circumcised, therefore children of both sexes should now be baptized. Surely, if baptism came in place of circumcision, its administration should be confined to the male sex; but it is by divine authority administered to believers of the other sex, and therefore it did not come in place of circumcision. Pedobaptists must admit that, so far as female infants are concerned, baptism did not take the place of circumcision; for circumcision occupied no *place*, and therefore could not be *displaced* by anything else. This is so plain as to need no elaboration.

3. *The eighth day was appointed for the circumcision of infants.*

Is this true of infant baptism? The thing itself is not commanded, to say nothing of the time. But Pedobaptists must be met on their own ground. They say that baptism has come "in the room of circumcision." If they believe this, consistency requires that they baptize male infants alone, and that they be baptized on the eighth day. Do they pursue this course? They do not; and their failure to do so may well excite doubt whether they are perfectly satisfied with their position.

4. *The Council of apostles, elders, and brethren at Jerusalem virtually denied the substitution of baptism for circumcision.*

In Acts xv. we have an account of this Council. The reason for its convocation was this: "Certain men" went from Judea to Antioch and "taught the brethren," saying, "Except ye be circumcised after the manner of Moses, ye cannot be saved." Paul and Barnabas joined issue with these "men," and after much disputation it was determined to send a deputation to Jerusalem to consult "the apostles and elders about this question." Paul and Barnabas belonged to this deputation, and upon their arrival at Jerusalem, *before the Council met,* some of the believing Pharisees urged the necessity of circumcision. The same question, therefore, was agitated both at Antioch and at Jerusalem. That question was whether the believing Gentiles ought to be circumcised. The Council met, and after due deliberation and consultation "it pleased the apostles and elders, with the whole church," to decide against the circumcision of Gentiles. Now, if baptism came in place of circumcision, the apostles knew it, and this was the time to declare it. A simple statement of the fact would have superseded all discussion. Why did they not say, "Circumcision is unnecessary, because baptism has taken its place"? This is what Pedobaptists would have said if they had been in that Council. The inspired apostles, however, did not say it. Indeed, the decision of the Council had reference to the believing Gentiles alone, and the understanding evidently was that believing Jews were at liberty to circumcise their children. This we may learn from Acts xxi. 17–25, and it is a fact utterly irreconcilable with the substitution of baptism for circumcision. When circumcision was regarded as a mark to designate nationality, Paul made no objection to it; but when its necessity to salvation was urged, he considered the great doctrine of justification by faith in Christ disparaged and shorn of its glory. To all circumcised with this latter view he said: "If ye be circumcised, Christ shall profit you nothing" (Gal. v. 2). But to return to the Council at Jerusalem: If baptism came in place of circumcision, the very reason which called that Council together must have led to a declaration of the fact, and it is strangely unaccountable that it did not. We are forced to the conclusion that baptism was not, in apostolic times, believed to be a substitute for circumcision. Hence the Council at Jerusalem could not, and did not, say it was. Its decision involved a virtual denial of the very thing for which Pedobaptists so strenuously contend.

I have now given a specimen—and but a specimen —of the considerations which show that baptism has not taken the place of circumcision. A volume might be written on this one point; but it is needless. He who is not convinced by the facts already presented would not be convinced "though one should rise from the dead."

The Scripture argument on infant baptism is now closed. I have examined the New-Testament claim of infants to baptism, and also the Old-Testament claim, and can perceive no mark of validity in either. My readers will therefore allow me to endorse what the *North British Review,* the organ of the Free (Presbyterian) Church of Scotland, says in its number for August, 1852:

"SCRIPTURE KNOWS NOTHING OF THE BAPTISM OF INFANTS."

SECTION IX.

The historical argument examined.

From the word of God, Pedobaptists go to church history and seek "aid and comfort" from its records. What does church history say of infant baptism? Much, I admit; but there is no proof that it was practised before the latter part of the second century. The proof is by no means conclusive that it was practised before the third century. This the reader will see as historical facts are presented.

I quote from Dr. Wall of the Church of England, whose *History of Infant Baptism* is in high repute wherever the English language is spoken. Referring, in chap. iii., to the well-known passage in Irenæus, he says, "Since this is the first express mention that we have met with of infants baptized, it is worth the while to look back and consider how near this man was to the apostles' time." Irenæus, according to Dr. Wall's chronology, lived about the year 167. It is well to give the disputed passage. Here it is: "For he [Christ] came to save all persons by himself: all, I mean, who by him are regenerated [or baptized] unto God; infants, and little ones, and children, and youths, and elder persons. Therefore he went through every age; for infants being an infant, sanctifying infants," etc. It is needless to quote further, for the controversy is about the meaning of the word "regenerated." It will be observed that Dr. Wall interpolates "baptized" as its meaning. *Renascor* is the word used in the Latin translation; for the original Greek is lost. That *renascor* means "born again" or "regenerated" is beyond dispute; nor is it necessary to deny that the "Fathers," so called, sometimes use it as synonymous with "baptized." Baptists, however, deny that it has this meaning in the passage under consideration, and distinguished Pedobaptists agree with them, as the following quotations prove.

The learned Winer, speaking of infant baptism, says, "Irenæus does not mention it, as has been supposed." *

Dr. Doddridge says, "We have only a Latin translation of this work; and some critics have supposed this passage spurious, or, allowing it to be genuine, it will not be granted that *to be regenerate* always in his writings signifies ' baptized.' " †

Pedobaptists must deeply feel their need of something to sustain their practice when they attempt to extort from Irenæus testimony in favor of infant bap-

* *Christian Review*, vol. iii., p. 213.
† *Miscellaneous Works*, p. 493,

tism. He says nothing about baptism in connection with infants.

Tertullian, who lived about the year 200, is often referred to by Pedobaptists as the first opponent of infant baptism, but they argue that his opposition proves the existence of the practice. It is by no means certain that Tertullian refers to the baptism of infants. The term which he uses, and which Dr. Wall translates "little children," is *parvulos.* Irenæus speaks of *infantes, parvulos.* He makes a distinction between *infantes* and *parvulos.* If Tertullian uses the latter term as Irenæus did, he does not refer to the baptism of unconscious infants, but to the baptism of "little children." These "little children" may have been capable of exercising faith in Christ. Whether they were or not I do not undertake to decide. It is true, however, that Tertullian, owing to his peculiar views, advised a delay of baptism on the part of certain classes of persons who had reached mature years.

Having come down to the beginning of the third century, may I not say that if infant baptism rests for its support on the practice of the first two centuries, it rests on a foundation of sand? To the end of two hundred years it has no distinct historical recognition.

From Tertullian, Dr. Wall comes to Origen, whom he represents as living about the year 210. Origen

DISTINCTIVE PRINCIPLES OF BAPTISTS. 75

wrote in Greek, and his works in the original were chiefly lost and Latin translations remain. Dr. Wall says "only the Latin translations." However this may be, he tells us that "upon the renewal of learning" nothing was admitted to be Origen's except translations made "into Latin either by *St. Hierom* * or *Rufinus*." He accords fidelity to Hierom in his translations, but says that "Rufinus altered or left out anything that he thought not orthodox." Nor is this all; for these significant words are added: "Whereas now in these Translations of *Rufinus* the reader *is uncertain* (as *Erasmus* angrily says) *whether he read* Origen or Rufinus." †

Dr. Wall admits that Origen's *Homilies on Leviticus* and his *Comments on the Epistle to the Romans* were translated by Rufinus; and in these productions we are supposed to have his strongest testimony in favor of infant baptism. In his eighth Homily he is represented as saying, "Infants also are, *by the usage of the church*, baptized." In his comments on Romans this language is attributed to him: "The church had *from the apostles a tradition* [or order] to give baptism even to infants." This is Dr. Wall's translation. He was

---

* Same as "Jerome."

† *History of Infant Baptism*, chap. v. In quoting from Dr. Wall I refer to chapters rather than to pages, because his *History* is published in different forms. I have the edition of 1705.

very anxious to translate the Latin term *traditio* "order." It seems, however, that he had some misgiving, and therefore put the word "order" in brackets. Let it not be forgotten that the translation of these portions of Origen's works was made from Greek into Latin by Rufinus, who "altered or left out anything that he thought not orthodox." Who knows, therefore—who can ever know—whether Origen wrote what is here ascribed to him? What alterations were made in his writings? Such as Rufinus, in his orthodoxy, thought proper. What things were "left out"? Only those that Rufinus *thought* ought to be left out! Erasmus, a prodigy of learning in his day, was uncertain whether he read "Origen or Rufinus." But if Origen did say what Rufinus represents him as saying, what does it amount to? Absolutely nothing with those who recognize the word of God as the only rule of faith and practice. The "usage of the church" and "a tradition from the apostles" are referred to as authority for infant baptism; there is no appeal to the Holy Scriptures. Who but a Romanist is willing to practise infant baptism as a tradition, and not a divine ordinance? Origen's testimony is valuable to a Papist, entirely worthless to a Protestant.

Leaving the "uncertain" writings of Origen, Dr. Wall conducts us into the Council of Carthage, in the year 253. This Council was composed of sixty-six bishops, or pastors, and Cyprian presided over it. One of the questions submitted to its decision was whether a child should be baptized before it was eight days old. Fidus, who presented the question, was in the negative; and rightly too, if the law of circumcision was to regulate the matter. The very fact that such a question was sent to the Council shows that infant baptism was a new thing. Had it been practised from the days of the apostles, the point whether a child should be baptized before the eighth day would have been settled before A. D. 253. The Council decided against the delay of baptism, assigning this weighty reason: "As far as in us lies, no soul, if possible, is to be lost." Here it will be seen that the necessity of baptism, in order to salvation, is recognized. In this supposed necessity infant baptism, doubtless, had its origin. This will be clear when the testimony of the great Neander is presented. The Council of Carthage attempted to justify infant baptism by referring to the fact that when the son of the Shunammite widow (2 Kings iv.) died, the prophet Elisha so stretched himself on the child as to apply his face to the child's face, his feet to the child's feet, etc. By this, said the Council, "spiritual equality is intimated"—that is, a child is spiritually equal to a grown person! A conclusive reason for infant baptism, truly! The cause must be desperate, indeed, when the decision of a

Council that could gravely advance such a conceit as an argument is invoked to sustain it.*

It is not necessary to refer to other of the so-called "Christian Fathers," especially to Augustine, as testifying in favor of infant baptism; for Baptists do not deny that infants were baptized from the days of Cyprian. Augustine, who died A. D. 430, refers to infant baptism as an apostolic tradition: *apostolica traditio* is the phrase he employs. He meant, no doubt, that it was handed down from the apostles by tradition that infants were to be baptized. This implies the silence of the New Testament on the subject. No one would say that it was handed down by tradition that believers are to be baptized. Why? Because the baptism of believers is so clearly taught that tradition is precluded. Not so as to infant baptism; for here there is room for tradition, because in regard to this rite the Scriptures are as silent as the grave. As to Augustine himself, the tradition to which he refers was not sufficiently operative to secure his baptism in infancy, though his mother, Monica, was a pious woman. He was not baptized till thirty years of age.

It has been intimated that the testimony of the great church historian Neander is decisive as to the

---

* The reader who wishes to verify the statements here made concerning the Council of Carthage may refer to Wall's *History*, chap. vi.

origin of infant baptism in its supposed necessity in order to salvation. He says, "That not till so late a period as (at least, certainly not earlier than) Irenæus a trace of infant baptism appears, and that it first became recognized as an apostolic tradition in the course of the third century, is evidence rather *against* than *for* the admission of its apostolic origin; specially since, in the spirit of the age when Christianity appeared, there were many elements which must have been favorable to the introduction of infant baptism—the same elements from which proceeded the notion of the magical effects of outward baptism, the notion of its absolute necessity for salvation, the notion which gave rise to the mythus [myth] that the apostles baptized the Old-Testament saints in Hades. How very much must infant baptism have corresponded with such a tendency if it had been favored by tradition!"*

Dr. Wall in the second part of his *History*, chap. vi., referring to the "ancient Fathers," says, "They differ concerning the future state of infants dying unbaptized; but all agreed that they missed of heaven."

In view of this testimony of two Pedobaptists of great celebrity, who does not see that infant baptism originated from its supposed inseparable connection with salvation? A deplorable misconception of the truth of the gospel gave it birth, while misappre-

* *Planting and Training of the Church*, p. 102.

hension of the teachings of the New Testament prolongs its injurious existence. The "historical argument" for infant baptism affords very little "aid and comfort" to Pedobaptists. But suppose it was a thousand times stronger; suppose every writer from the death of the last apostle had expressed himself in favor of it; even then it would be nothing less than an act of will-worship while the Scriptures are silent concerning it. The perplexing question, "Who hath required this at your hands?" should confound its advocates. "The Bible, the Bible alone," said Chillingworth, "is the religion of Protestants." Arguments from antiquity, to be available, must penetrate the antiquity of the apostolic age and rest on the teachings of the New Testament. All other arguments are worthless.

SECTION X.

Objections to infant baptism.

In view of the considerations presented in the preceding pages, there must be very serious objections to infant baptism. Some of these objections will now be considered.

1. *A decided objection to it is that its advocates cannot agree why it should be practised.*

How conflicting, how antagonistic, their opinions! Roman Catholics baptize infants, in order to their salvation. They consider baptism essential to the salvation of both adults and infants. They have sometimes shown the sincerity of their belief by attempting to baptize children before they were born. Episcopalians, in accepting the teachings of the "Book of Common Prayer," baptize infants to make them children of God by regeneration. John Calvin, as may be seen in his *Life* by Henry (vol. i., pp. 82, 83), maintains that infants are capable of exercising faith, and that their baptism is an exemplification of believers' baptism. This seems also to have been Martin Luther's opinion. John Wesley in his *Treatise on Baptism* says, " If infants are guilty of original sin, they are proper subjects of baptism, seeing, in the ordinary way, that they cannot be saved, unless this be washed away in baptism." The "Directory" of the Westminster Assembly places the right of the infants of believers to baptism on the ground that they are "federally holy." The opinion held by probably the larger number of Protestant Pedobaptists is that infants are baptized "to bring them into the church." But Dr. Samuel Miller, as we have seen, insists that the children of Christian parents are born members of the church, and are baptized because they are members: while Dr. Summers derives the right of infants to baptism from "their personal connection with the Second Adam."

These are specimens of the reasons urged in favor of infant baptism. How contradictory! How antagonistic! It seems that infants are to be baptized that they may be saved; that they may be regenerated; because they have faith; because their parents are believers; because they are involved in original sin; because they are holy; because they ought to be brought into the church; because they are in the church by virtue of their birth; and because of their "personal connection" with Christ, in consequence of his assumption of human nature. It would be well for the various sects of Pedobaptists to call a Council to decide why infants should be baptized. The reasons in favor of the practice are at present so contradictory and so self-destructive that it must involve the advocates of the system in great perplexity. Many, though, would object to such a Council because, for obvious reasons, the Pope of Rome should preside over it, and others would object because it would probably be in session as long as the Council of Trent. Still, if one good reason could be furnished for infant baptism by the united wisdom of Romanists and Protestants, it would be more satisfactory than all the reasons which are now urged.

2. *A second objection to infant baptism is that its tendency is to unite the church and the world.*

Jesus Christ evidently designed the church to be the light of the world. His followers are not of the world, but are chosen out of the world. If anything in the

New Testament is plain, it is plain that the Lord Jesus intended that there should be a line of demarcation between the church and the world. It is needless to argue a point so clear. Now, the tendency of infant baptism is to unite the church and the world, and thus to obliterate the line of demarcation which the Saviour has established. Let the principles of Pedobaptism universally prevail, and one of three things will inevitably follow—either there will be no church, or there will be no world, or there will be a *worldly church*. The universal prevalence of Pedobaptist sentiments would bring all " born of the flesh " into the church. To be *born,* not to be *born again*, would be the qualification for membership. The unregenerate members would be in a large majority. The world would absorb the church, or, to say the least, there would be an intensely worldly church. Is this not true of the national churches of Europe? The time has been, whatever may be the case now, when in England "partaking of the Lord's Supper" preceded the holding of the civil and military offices of the kingdom. Thus a premium was offered for hypocrisy, and many an infidel availed himself of it. In the United States of America there are so many counteracting influences that infant baptism cannot *fully* develop its tendency to unite the church and the world. Indeed, in some respects, Pedobaptists practically repudiate their own principles. They do not treat their "baptized children" as church-members. If they did, there would be a deplorable state of things. The unregenerate members of local congregations would generally be in the majority, and would exert a controlling influence.

3. *Another objection to infant baptism is that it cherishes in "baptized children" the delusive belief that they are better than others; that their salvation is more hopeful.*

In many instances, it is to be feared, they are led to consider themselves in a saved state. The children of Romanists must so regard themselves if they attribute to baptism the efficacy ascribed to it by Papists. If the children of Episcopalians believe the "Book of Common Prayer," they must grow up under the false persuasion that in their baptism they "were made members of Christ, children of God, and inheritors of the kingdom of heaven." If the children of Methodists believe the "Discipline," and that the prayer offered at their baptism was heard, they must recognize themselves as baptized not only "with water," but "with the Holy Ghost." If the children of Presbyterians believe the "Westminster Confession" and the "Directory," they look upon themselves as "federally holy"—"in covenant with God"—and consider that "the covenant was sealed by their baptism." Will not all these classes of children imagine themselves better than others? Will they not, under the teaching they receive, view other children as consigned to the "uncovenanted mercies" of God, while they occupy a high vantage-ground? Will not their delusive belief present a serious obstacle in the way of their salvation? Is there any rational probability of their salvation, unless they disbelieve the dogmas inculcated in their baptism? Will the children of Roman Catholics ever be saved while they regard their baptism as having placed them in a saved state? Will the children of Episcopalians become the "children of God" so long as they entertain the absurd notion that they were made his children by baptism? Will the children of Methodists be regenerated while they imagine that they have been baptized "with the Holy Ghost"? Will the children of Presbyterians repent and acknowledge their guilt and condemnation before God while they lay the "flattering unction to their souls" that they are "federally holy" and "in covenant with God"?

I would not give offence, but must say that Pedobaptist children must take the first step in the pursuit of salvation by practically denying the truth of what they have been taught concerning their baptism. It will be asked, Are not thousands of the children of Pedobaptists converted to God? I gladly concede it;

but why is it so? One prominent reason, doubtless, is that, on the part of their ministers and parents, there is a practical repudiation of their baptismal theories. The "baptized children," whatever the baptismal formulas may say, are taught that they are sinners, unregenerate, lost, condemned, and exposed to the wrath of God, for the very reason that they are not "in covenant" with him. Thanks be to God that the preaching and teaching of Pedobaptists do not accord with their "Creeds," so far as the subject of infant baptism is concerned! The discrepancy is vital to the welfare of their offspring. There are some happy inconsistencies.

4. *A fourth objection to infant baptism is that it interferes with the independent action of the minds of "baptized children" on the subject of baptism, and in numberless instances prevents baptism on a profession of faith in Christ.*

Suppose, when "baptized children" reach mature years, they are, as is often the case, annoyed with doubts concerning the validity of their baptism. They feel at once that they cannot entertain these doubts without virtually calling in question the propriety of what their parents caused to be done for them in their infancy. Filial respect and reverence present almost insuperable barriers in the way of an impartial investigation of the subject. The question comes up, Shall we *reflect* on the wisdom of our parents by declaring their act null and void? If the parents are dead and gone to be with Christ, the difficulty is often greater. The question then assumes this form: Shall we repudiate what our now-glorified parents did for us in our infancy? It often requires a great struggle to surmount the difficulty, and in many cases it is never surmounted. It is unquestionably true that the influence of infant baptism interferes with the unbiased action of many minds with regard to scriptural baptism. How great would be the number of those who, but for their infant baptism so called, would be baptized on a profession of faith in Christ! They hesitate to say that the "infantile rite" was worthless. They know that great and good men have practised infant baptism. Their minds are perplexed. They wish it had so happened that they had not been baptized in infancy. Still, the sprinkling of the baptismal (!) waters on them in infancy now prevents an intelligent immersion into Christ on a profession of faith in his name. Is it not an objection to infant baptism that it prevents so many from obeying Christ, and even fosters a spirit of disobedience?

5. *As a last objection to infant baptism, I refer to its tendency to supplant believers' baptism and banish it from the world.*

This objection, though presented last, is first in importance. It is, indeed, the capital objection, and if exhibited in all its phases would virtually embrace all objections. It is not, however, necessary to dwell on it at length, because its force and conclusiveness are readily seen. By all who practise baptism at all it is admitted that the New Testament enjoins the baptism of believers in Christ. The universality of this admission precludes the necessity of proof. The baptism of believers, then, is a divine ordinance. Is it reasonable to suppose that two divine ordinances antagonize with each other? Is it credible that this is the case? Pedobaptists say that infant baptism is a divine ordinance, and they are slow to admit that it antagonizes with the baptism of believers. But the antagonism is direct, positive. The inevitable tendency of infant baptism is to supplant the baptism of believers. This is owing to the fact that it is practically regarded by Pedobaptists as superseding the necessity of believers' baptism. It must be so regarded, or it is made null and void. When baptized infants grow up to maturity and become believers in Christ, there is nothing said among Pedobaptists about baptism on a profession of faith. No; the baptism of the unconscious infant is allowed to prevent the baptism of the intelligent believer. Hence it is easy to see the tendency of infant baptism to supplant and banish the baptism of believers from the world. A supposition will make this so plain that no one can misunderstand it: Let it be supposed, then, that the principles of Pedobaptists prevail throughout the world. All parents come into the church and have their children baptized in infancy. If this supposition were realized, where would believers' baptism be? It would in one generation be utterly supplanted and banished from the world. An ordinance established by Christ to be observed to the end of time would be abolished. There would be no scriptural baptism on earth. One of the institutions of the Head of the church would not be permitted to have a place in the world which he made, and in which he labored, toiled suffered, and died! How startling and fearful is this! A human tradition arraying itself against an ordinance of Heaven, and attempting to destroy it and leave no memorial of its existence on the face of the globe!

Influenced by the considerations presented in the ten sections of this chapter, Baptists regard infant baptism as utterly destitute of scriptural support; and, in view of its many evils, they are most decided in their opposition to it. On the other hand, they are the earnest advocates of the baptism of believers in Christ; and of believers alone. In this opposition and in this advocacy may be seen one of the prominent DISTINCTIVE PRINCIPLES OF BAPTISTS.

CHAPTER II.

BAPTISTS CONSIDER THE IMMERSION IN WATER OF A BELIEVER IN CHRIST ESSENTIAL TO BAPTISM —SO ESSENTIAL THAT WITHOUT IT THERE IS NO BAPTISM.

SECTION I.

Greek lexicons give " immerse," " dip," or " plunge" as the primary, ordinary, and literal meaning of " baptizo."

IN the common version of the Scriptures *baptizo* and *baptisma* are *Anglicized*, but not translated. This is invariably true of the latter term, and it is true of the former whenever the ordinance of baptism is referred to. *Baptismos* is used four times. In three instances it has no reference to the baptismal ordinance, and is translated " washing ;" which washing was evidently the result of immersion. In the other instance it is Anglicized. *Bapto,* from which *baptizo* is derived, is employed in the Greek New Testament three times, and *embapto* three times. Both are translated " dip " in the common version. There is no more difference in their meaning than there is between the word " dip " and the phrase " dip in."

These verbs are never used in connection with baptism as a religious ordinance; *baptizo* is the verb always used.

I have referred to *baptizo* and *baptisma* as Anglicized words. By this it is meant that their termination is made to correspond with the termination of English words. In *baptizo* the final letter is changed into *e*, and in *baptisma* the last letter is dropped altogether. To make this matter of Anglicism perfectly plain, it is only necessary to say that if the Greek *rantizo*, meaning "sprinkle," had been Anglicized, we should have "rantize" in the New Testament wherever we now have "sprinkle."

The version of the Bible now in common use was made by order of King James I. of England, and was first published in the year 1611. The king gave a number of rules for the guidance of his translators, and the third rule virtually forbids the translation of "baptize" and "baptism." This third rule is as follows: "The old ecclesiastical words to be kept, as the word 'church' not to be translated 'congregation.'" It is absurd to say that this rule had exclusive reference to the term "church," for this term is manifestly given as a specimen of "old ecclesiastical words;" and why should "words" be mentioned if the rule was to be applied to but one word? The question, then, is, Are "baptism" and "baptize" "old ecclesiastical words"? They were *words* when the Bible was translated, or they would not be found in it. They had been used by church historians and by writers on ecclesiastical law, and were, therefore, *ecclesiastical.* They had been in use a long time, and were, consequently, *old.* They were "old ecclesiastical words," such words as the king commanded "to be kept"— "not to be translated." It is worthy of notice, too, that the Bishop of London, at the king's instance, wrote to the translators, reminding them that His Majesty wished his *"third* and *fourth* rule" to be specially observed.* This circumstance must have called particular attention to the rule under consideration. In view of these facts, it may surely be said that the translators knew what were "old ecclesiastical words." Let their testimony, then, be adduced. In their "Preface to the Reader" they say that they had, "on the one side, avoided the scrupulosity of the Puritans, who left the old ecclesiastical words and betook them to other, as when they put 'washing' for 'baptism' and 'congregation' for 'church;' and, on the other hand, had shunned the obscurity of the Papists." Is not this enough? Here there is not only an admission that "baptism" was included in the "old ecclesiastical words," but this admission is made by the translators themselves—made most cheerfully, for it

---

*See Lewis's *History of Translations,* pp. 317, 319.

was made in condemnation of the Puritans and in commendation of themselves.

The position that King James virtually forbade the translation of "baptize" and "baptism" is established by the foregoing considerations; but to give it additional strength I refer to the king's fourth rule, as follows: "When any word hath divers significations, *that* to be kept which hath been most commonly used by the most eminent Fathers, being agreeable to the propriety of the place and the analogy of faith. Suppose I were to admit, for argument's sake, what some Pedobaptists insist on—namely, that *baptizo* has divers significations. What then? Every man of intelligence knows that from the days of the apostles to the reign of King James "immerse" was its commonly-received meaning. Was not immersion ordinarily practised for *thirteen hundred years?* Dr. Whitby, Dr. Wall, Professor Moses Stuart, and I know not how many other Pedobaptists of distinction, make this concession. Far be it from me to say that *baptizo* is a word of "divers significations;" but even if it were, the king's translators, if they had translated it at all, would have been compelled to render it "immerse," for it was "most commonly used" in this sense by "the most eminent Fathers." But it will be seen that the king's *third* rule makes inoperative his *fourth,* so far as "old ecclesiastical words" are concerned. Whether such words have one meaning or a thousand meanings, they are "to be kept"—"not to be translated." The translators were not at liberty to refer to the signification immemorially attached by the Greeks to *baptizo*—a signification which received the cordial endorsement of "the most eminent Fathers." They might have examined the endorsement if the royal decree had not said, "*Hitherto, but no farther*"—"the old ecclesiastical words to be kept."

The fact that "baptize" is an Anglicized, and not a translated, word makes an appeal to Greek lexicons necessary to ascertain its meaning. Lexicons, it is true, do not constitute the *ultimate* authority, but their testimony is highly important. I have made it a point to examine all the lexicons I have seen (and they have been many) concerning the import of *baptizo*. There is among them a remarkable unanimity in representing "immerse," or its equivalent, as the primary and ordinary meaning of the word. According to lexicographers, it is a word of definite import—as much so as any other. It is as specific as *rantizo*, and it might be argued just as plausibly that *rantizo* means "to immerse" as that *baptizo* means "to sprinkle." I have seen no lexicon that gives "sprinkle" as a meaning of *baptizo*, and but one that makes "to pour upon" one of its significations. In the first edition of Liddell & Scott's Greek-and-English lexicon "to pour upon" is given as the seventh meaning of *baptizo*. It is a significant fact, however, that, while passages in classic Greek authors are referred to as illustrative of the ordinary meaning of the word, there is no mention of any passage that sustains the definition "to pour upon."

It is worthy of special remark that the second edition of Liddell & Scott does not contain the phrase "to pour upon." This is an important fact, of which Baptists may avail themselves. It has been well said by a scholar now dead:* "When it is remembered that the definition 'pour upon' was assigned to *baptizo* in the first English edition, on the authority of Francis Passow, whose German work forms the basis of that of Liddell & Scott, this change in the second English edition is an admission as gratifying to Baptists as it is unwelcome to their opponents. Messrs. Liddell & Scott, who cannot be charged with a leaning to Baptist sentiments, have deliberately, after due examination, withdrawn their authority in favor of 'pour upon' as a signification of the verb *baptizo*, and now define the word just as Baptist scholars have defined it after a careful study of the passages in which it occurs in the Greek authors. Of such a concession Baptists know well how to take advantage."

I now repeat that there is among lexicons a perfect

* Rev. W. C. Duncan, D. D.

concurrence in assigning "immerse" or its equivalent as the primary and ordinary meaning of *baptizo*. This ought to settle the baptismal controversy. For what says Blackstone, who is almost the idol of the legal profession?—"Words are generally to be understood in their usual and most known signification; not so much regarding the propriety of grammar as their general and popular use." * "Immerse" was the "usual and most known signification" of *baptizo* among the Greeks. It was its "general and popular use," as we shall see in the proper place.

To return to the argument derived from lexicons: All English dictionaries give "immerse" or its equivalent as the ordinary meaning of "dip." It would, therefore, be very unreasonable to deny that "dip" ordinarily means "to immerse." Greek lexicons give "immerse" as the ordinary meaning of *baptizo*. Is it not, then, just as unreasonable to deny that *baptizo* ordinarily means "to immerse" as it would be to deny that "dip" has this signification? Indeed, there is no argument employed by Pedobaptists to divest *baptizo* of its usual meaning which may not as plausibly be employed to divest "dip" of its ordinary import; for, though "dip" is a definite and specific word, *baptizo* is more so. We speak of "the *dip* of the magnetic needle" and of "the dip of a stratum in

---

* Sharswood's *Blackstone*, vol., i. p. 58.

geology," while Pope uses the expression "dipping into a volume of history." If Pedobaptists could find *baptizo* in such connections, there would be rejoicing from Dan to Beersheba. The man who would attempt to prove that "dip" means "to sprinkle" or "pour" would probably be laughed at; but he could make a more plausible effort in adducing his proof than if he were to attempt to prove the same thing concerning *baptizo*. Let us see: Such a man might say that Johnson, Webster, and Worcester in their large dictionaries give "moisten" and "wet" as meanings of "dip," and refer as authority to Milton, who uses the following words: "A cold shuddering dew *dips* me all over." Talking with himself, such a reasoner might say, "It is a fixed fact that 'dip' means 'to moisten' and 'wet.' Who will dispute what Johnson, Webster, and Worcester say, sustained as they are by the 'prince of British poets'? Very well. 'Dip' means to 'moisten' and 'wet.' Everybody knows that a thing can be moistened or made wet by having water poured or sprinkled on it. Therefore, 'dip' means 'to pour' and 'sprinkle.'" Now, I affirm that this argument is more plausible than any I ever heard from a Pedobaptist to prove that *baptizo* means "pour" and "sprinkle;" yet it is replete with sophistry. It assumes as true the fallacy that if a process can be accomplished in two different ways, the two verbs employed to denote those two ways mean the same thing. An object may be moistened by being dipped in water, but "moisten" and "dip" are not synonymous. The same object may be moistened by having water sprinkled or poured on it, but neither "moisten and sprinkle," nor "moisten and pour," are identical in import. Though the moistening may *result* from the dipping, sprinkling, or pouring, the three acts are clearly distinguishable, and definite terms are used to express them.

It is proper to say of the Greek lexicons to which I have referred that they were all made by men who had no partialities for Baptists. A regard for truth, therefore, and no desire to give currency to the practice of immersion, elicited from them the definition they have given of *baptizo*. Baptists may well felicitate themselves that their opponents bear this strong testimony.

SECTION II.

Distinguished Pedobaptist scholars and theologians admit that "baptizo" means "to immerse."

Here I shall probably be told that it is unfair to take advantage of Pedobaptist concessions. There is, however, nothing unfair in such a course. No one can say that there is without calling in question the propriety of what Paul did in his great discourse at

Athens; for he availed himself of the declaration of a Greek poet, and made the poetic statement a part of his argument. I shall aim to do nothing that is not justified by the example of the great apostle. Pedobaptist concessions are of great value, for it may be said, in the language of another on a different matter, "This testimony of theirs, to me, is worth a thousand others, seeing it comes from such as, in my opinion, *are evidently interested to speak quite otherwise.*"

The reader's earnest attention is called to the following extracts.

I begin with John Calvin, a learned Presbyterian, who lived more than three hundred years ago. He was very decided in his opposition to Baptists, or "Anabaptists," as he contemptuously styled them. He wrote in Latin, and I avail myself of the translation of John Allen, published by the Presbyterian Board of Publication, Philadelphia. In his *Institutes* (vol. ii., book iv., chap. xv., paragraph 19, p. 491) he says, "But whether the person who is baptized be wholly immersed, and whether thrice or once, or whether water be only poured or sprinkled upon him, is of no importance; churches ought to be left at liberty, in this respect, to act according to the difference of countries. The very word *baptize*, however, signifies 'to immerse;' and it is certain that immersion was the practice of the ancient Church."

It will be seen that Calvin expresses two *opinions* and states two *facts*. The *opinions* are that it is of no importance how water is used, and that churches should be free to decide as they please; the *facts* are that "baptize" means "to immerse," and that immersion was the practice of the ancient church. With Calvin's *opinions* I have nothing to do, but his *facts* claim attention. What "baptize" means is a question of fact, and must be decided by testimony. So of the practice of the ancient church. Calvin gave his verdict on the testimony establishing the facts. The reader will observe the distinction between opinions and facts.

Dr. George Campbell, a learned Presbyterian of Scotland, who lived about a hundred years ago, in his notes on Matt. iii. 11, says, "The word *baptizein*" (infinitive mode, present tense, of *baptizo*), "both in sacred authors and in classical, signifies 'to dip,' 'to plunge,' 'to immerse,' and was rendered by Tertullian, the oldest of the Latin Fathers, *tingere*—the term used for dyeing cloth, which was by immersion. It is always construed suitably to this meaning." In his *Lectures on Systematic Theology and Pulpit Eloquence* he expresses himself, in Lecture X., as follows: "Another error in disputation which is by far too common is when one will admit nothing in the plea or arguments of an adversary to be of the smallest we'ght. . . . I have heard a disputant of this stamp, in defiance of etymology and use, maintain that the word rendered in the New Testament 'baptize' means, more properly, 'to sprinkle' than 'to plunge,' and, in defiance of all antiquity, that the former method was the earliest, and for many centuries the most general, practice in baptizing. One who argues in this manner never fails, with persons of knowledge, to betray the cause he would defend; and though, with respect to the vulgar, bold assertions generally succeed as well as arguments—sometimes better—yet a candid mind will disdain to take the help of a falsehood even in support of the truth."

Dr. Thomas Chalmers, for many years regarded by all as the greatest Presbyterian theologian of Scotland, and by some as the greatest theologian of the world in his day, uses the following language: "The original meaning of the word 'baptism' is 'immersion;' and, though we regard it as a point of indifferency whether the ordinance so named be performed in this way or by sprinkling, yet we doubt not that the prevalent style of the administration in the apostles' days was by an actual submerging of the whole body under water. We advert to this for the purpose of throwing light on the analogy that is instituted on these verses. Jesus Christ, by death, underwent this sort of baptism —even immersion under the surface of the ground, whence he soon emerged again by his resurrection We, by being baptized into his death, are conceived to have made a similar translation."*

Professor Moses Stuart, the most renowned Congregationalist of his day, and the ornament of the Theological Seminary of Andover, Massachusetts, in his treatise on the *Mode of Baptism* (p. 14), says: †
"*Bapto* and *baptizo* mean 'to dip,' 'plunge,' or 'immerge' into anything liquid. All lexicographers and critics of any note are agreed in this. My proof of this position, then, need not necessarily be protracted; but for the sake of ample confirmation I must beg the reader's patience while I lay before him, as briefly as may be, the results of an investigation which seems to leave no room for doubt."

I will also give the testimony of an eminent man who has recently died. Dean Stanley, in an article on "Baptism" in the *Nineteenth Century* for October, 1879, says: "For the first thirteen centuries the almost universal practice of baptism was that of which we read in the New Testament, and which is the very meaning of the word 'baptize'—that those who were baptized were plunged, submerged, immersed, into the water."

But why proceed farther with the testimony of distinguished Pedobaptist scholars and theologians?

---

* *Lectures on Romans*, Lecture XXX., on chap. vi. 3-7.

† This is a reprint from the *Biblical Repository*, vol. iii., No. 11.

What I have adduced is surely sufficient. These witnesses testify that *baptizo* means "to immerse;" nor do they say that it means "to sprinkle" and "pour." True it is that Calvin thought immersion *or* sprinkling a matter of "no importance," and Chalmers regarded it as a "point of indifferency;" but they are both clear as to what the word *baptizo* means. This is all I want—their *testimony* as to the meaning of the word. Their *opinion* as to the admissibility of sprinkling I reject, for it is utterly gratuitous unless *baptizo* means "to sprinkle." This they did not say, and could not say. The distinction between a fact and an opinion deserves special notice. He who, acquainted with the *usus loquendi* of a term, testifies that it means a certain thing, bears witness to a *fact;* but if he says that it is not important to adhere to the meaning established by the *usus loquendi*, he expresses an *opinion*.

It may be asked why those Pedobaptist scholars who concede that *baptizo* means "to immerse" have not become practical immersionists. This is a question difficult to answer. That they ought to have shown their faith by their works does not admit a doubt. Some, perhaps, have failed to do so on account of early predilections; others have not felt willing to disturb their denominational relations; and others still have had a horror of the charge of fickleness. Probably, however, the greater number, like Professor Stuart, have persuaded themselves that, as the Christian Dispensation is eminently spiritual, it is a matter of little moment, provided the heart is right, as to a particular observance of "external rites." Such persons seem to forget that the way to show that the heart is right with God is to do the *very thing* he has commanded. The reasons suggested for the failure of those Pedobaptists who have made such concessions as have been quoted to do their duty are, I must say, unsatisfactory. Satisfactory reasons cannot be given, for impossibilities cannot be performed. Those who admit that Jesus Christ commanded his disciples to be immersed, and at the same time array themselves in practical opposition to immersion, are accountable to him. Here the matter must be left.

SECTION III.

The classical usage of "baptizo" establishes the position of Baptists.

I have said that lexicons are not the *ultimate* authority in settling the meaning of words. The truth of this statement can be readily seen. Lexicographers are necessarily dependent on the sense in which words are used to ascertain their meaning. But it is possible for them to mistake that sense. If they do, there is an appeal from their definitions to usage (called the *usus loquendi*), which is the ultimate authority. I shall now show how classic Greek authors used the word *baptizo*—not that I complain of the lexicons, but that I may show that the usage of the word fully justifies the lexicons in giving "immerse" or its equivalent as its primary, ordinary, literal meaning. It is pleasant o go back to the ultimate authority.

Few men ever examined the classical import of *baptizo* more extensively than the late Dr. Alexander Carson, and the result of his labors is before the public. Since his death Dr. T. J. Conant has gone more exhaustively into the subject, apparently leaving nothing more to be said. These accomplished scholars prove beyond question that *baptizo* was used by the Greeks in the sense of "immerse;" but, as I prefer not to quote from Baptist authors, I do not avail myself of the learned labors of Drs. Carson and Conant. For obvious reasons, I give the preference to Pedobaptist testimony. The following extracts, therefore, are made from Professor Stuart on the *Mode of Baptism*. He refers to a number of Greek authors.

PINDAR, who was born five hundred and twenty years before Christ, says : "*As when a net is cast into the sea the cork swims above, so am I* UNPLUNGED (*abaptistos*); on which the Greek scholiast, in commenting, says : As the cork (*ou dunei*) *does not sink*, so I am *abaptistos —unplunged, not immersed.* The cork remains *abap-*

tistos, and swims on the surface of the sea, being of a nature which is *abaptistos;* in like manner, I am *abaptistos.*"

Pindar was describing the utter incompetency of his enemies to *plunge* him into ruin. It is only necessary to say to the English scholar that the letter *a* (in Greek, "alpha"), prefixed in the foregoing extract to *baptistos*, conveys a negative idea. *Abaptistos*, therefore, means "unplunged," "undipped," "unimmersed." "Unsprinkled" or "unpoured" is perfectly out of the question.

HIPPOCRATES, who lived about four hundred and thirty years before the Christian era, says: "*Shall I not laugh at the man who* SINKS (*baptisanta*) *his ship by overloading it, and then complains of the sea for engulfing it with its cargo?*"

ARISTOTLE, who died three hundred and thirty-two years before Christ, "speaks of a saying among the Phenicians, that there were certain places, beyond the Pillars of Hercules, *which when it is ebb-tide are not* OVERFLOWED (*mee baptizesthai*)."

HERACLIDES PONTICUS, a disciple of Aristotle, says: "*When a piece of iron is taken red hot from the fire and* PLUNGED *in the water* (*hudati baptizetai*), *the heat, being quenched by the peculiar nature of the water, ceases.*"

DIODORUS SICULUS, who lived about the middle of

the century before Christ, uses these words: "*Most of the land-animals that are intercepted by the river* [Nile] *perish, being* OVERWHELMED." Again: "*The river, borne along by a more violent current,* OVERWHELMED (*ebaptise*) *many.*"

STRABO, the celebrated geographer, who died A. D. 25—a very short time before John the Baptist began to preach in the wilderness of Judea—"speaking of a lake near Agrigentum, says: Things that elsewhere cannot float DO NOT SINK (*mee baptizesthai*) in the water of this lake, but swim in the manner of wood." Again: "*If one shoots an arrow into the channel* [of a certain rivulet in Cappadocia], *the force of the water resists it so much that it will scarcely* PLUNGE IN (*baptizesthai*)." Again: "*They* [the soldiers] *marched a whole day through the water* PLUNGED IN (*baptizomenōn*) *up to the waist.*" Once more: "The bitumen floats on the top [of the lake Sirbon], because of the nature of the water, which admits of no diving; nor can any one who enters it PLUNGE IN (*baptizesthai*), but is borne up."

JOSEPHUS, who died A. D. 93, aged fifty-six, and was therefore contemporary with the apostles, "speaking of the ship in which Jonah was, says: *Mellontos baptizesthai tou skaphous*—*the ship being about* TO SINK." In the history of his own life, "speaking of a voyage to Rome, during which the ship that carried him foundered in the Adriatic, he says: *Our ship being* IMMERSED *or* SINKING *in the Adriatic*. Speaking of Aristobulus as having been drowned by command of Herod, he says: *The boy was sent to Jericho, and there, agreeably to command, being* IMMERSED *in a pond (baptizomenos en kolumbeethra), he perished.*"

PLUTARCH, who died about A. D. 140, refers to a Roman general "DIPPING (*baptisas*) his hand into blood," etc. Again: "PLUNGE (*baptison*) yourself into the sea."

LUCIAN, who died A. D. 180, represents Timon, the man-hater, as saying: "*If a winter's flood should carry away any one, and he, stretching out his hands, should beg for help, I would press down the head of such an one when* SINKING (*baptizonta*), *so that he could not rise again.*"

The reader, by referring to Professor Stuart's treatise on the *Mode of Baptism* (pp. 14–20), can test the accuracy of these quotations. I might add to their number, but these are sufficient. It will be seen that I have used Roman instead of Greek letters. This has been done for the satisfaction of a large majority of those who will read these pages.

"Immerse" is clearly the classical meaning of *baptizo*. In all the preceding extracts it might with propriety be employed. A "sinking ship," for example, is a ship about to be immersed. Nor is it any abuse of language to say that places "not overflowed" are not immersed. I solicit special attention to the fact that, of the Greek authors referred to, some lived before the coming of Christ, some during the apostolic age, and others at a period subsequent to that age. Seven hundred years intervened between the birth of Pindar and the death of Lucian. During those seven centuries usage shows that *baptizo* meant " to immerse." Most of the classic Greek writers lived before baptism was instituted, and knew nothing of immersion as a religious ordinance; those who lived after its institution cared nothing for it. There was no controversy as to the meaning of *baptizo* during the classic period of Grecian history; there was no motive, therefore, that could so influence Greek writers as to induce them to use the word in any but its authorized sense. That sense was most obviously "to immerse." Even Dr. Edward Beecher, though carried away with the notion that *baptizo*, "in its religious sense," means "to purify," admits that in classic usage it signifies "to immerse." He says: "I freely admit that in numerous cases it clearly denotes 'to immerse,' in which case an agent submerges partially or totally some person or thing. Indeed, this is so notoriously true that I need attempt no proof. Innumerable examples are at hand."[*]

No man of established reputation as a Greek scholar

---
[*] Beecher *On Baptism*, p. 9.

will deny that *baptizo*, at the beginning of the Christian era, meant "to immerse," and that usage had confirmed that meaning. Dr. Doddridge virtually admits this to be its import in the New Testament when used as descriptive of the sufferings of Christ. Hence he paraphrases Luke xii. 50 thus: "But I have, indeed, in the mean time, a most dreadful baptism to be baptized with, and know that I shall shortly be bathed, as it were, in blood, and *plunged* in the most *overwhelming* distress." * *Baptizo* literally means "immerse," and therefore in its figurative application it is used to denote an immersion in sorrow, suffering, and affliction.

But some say that though *baptizo*, in classic Greek, means "to immerse," it does not follow that it is to be understood in this sense in the New Testament. They discourse learnedly on the difference between classic and sacred Greek. They insist that *baptizo* has in the Scriptures a *theological* sense. In short, they forget what they have learned from Ernesti's *Principles of Interpretation*—namely, that "when God has spoken to men he has spoken in the language of men, for he has spoken by men and for men."

For the benefit of these ingenious critics, I quote from an able Methodist work on theology. The author is showing, in opposition to the Socinian view

* *Family Expositor*, p. 204.

DISTINCTIVE PRINCIPLES OF BAPTISTS. 111

that the apostles, in referring to the death of Christ, employ terms which convey the idea of expiation. He says: "The use to be made of this in the argument is that, as the apostles found the very terms they used with reference to the nature and efficacy of the death of Christ fixed in an expiatory signification among the Greeks, they could not, in honesty, use them in a distant figurative sense, much less in a contrary one, without due notice of their having invested them with a new import being given to their readers. . . . In like manner, the Jews had their expiatory sacrifices, and the terms and phrases used in them are, in like manner, employed by the apostles to characterize the death of their Lord; and they would have been as guilty of misleading their Jewish as their Gentile readers had they employed them in a new sense and without warning, which, unquestionably, they never gave." *

Dr. Hodge, in his *Way of Life*, expresses the same view.

To all this I cordially subscribe. The apostles found in use among the people certain terms which conveyed to their minds the idea of expiation. They used those terms, and evidently in that sense. As honest men they could not do otherwise without giving information of the fact. So reasons the accom-

* Richard Watson's *Theological Institutes*, vol. ii., p. 151.

plished Richard Watson. Very well. The same apostles found the term *baptizo* fixed in its meaning, and that meaning was "to immerse." Could they, then, "in honesty," employ it to denote "sprinkle" and "pour" without notifying their readers of the fact? Dr. Watson being judge, they could not. "Unquestionably," they never intimated to Jew or Gentile that they used the word in a new sense. Now, I insist that Methodists ought either to admit the validity of this argument in reference to *baptizo* or reject as inconclusive the reasoning against Socinians. It is to be remembered, also, that those who say that the *scriptural* meaning of *baptizo* differs from its *classic* meaning must prove it; the burden of proof is on them. If they say it means "to sprinkle," let them show it; if they affirm that it means "to pour," let them establish this signification. If Dr. Beecher can do anything for his "purification theory," let him do it. Baptists occupy a position which commends itself to every unprejudiced mind. They say that *baptizo*, among the Greeks, meant "to immerse," and that John the Baptist, Christ, and the apostles used it in the same sense and just as the people understood it.

I think it has now been shown that the classical meaning of *baptizo* is "immerse," and that it is perfectly gratuitous to assert that its scriptural meaning differs from its classical import.

SECTION IV.

The design of baptism furnishes an argument in favor of the position of Baptists.

In the ordinance of baptism there is a profession of faith in Jesus Christ, as we may learn from Eph. iv. 5: "One Lord, one faith, one baptism." The term "Lord" in this passage, as is generally the case in the Epistles, refers to Christ. He, having died and risen again, is presented in the gospel as the Object of faith and the Author of salvation. Faith is a trustful acceptance of Christ as the Saviour. On a profession of this "one faith" in the "one Lord," the "one baptism" is administered. Baptism is therefore a profession of faith. Take away the "one Lord," and the "one faith" becomes vain, for there is no object of faith; and the "one baptism" is vain also, for there is no faith of which it is the profession. If we transpose the terms of the passage, we see that the transposition is ruinous. If we put faith before the Lord, and baptism before faith, we invert the inspired order. If changed, the order is virtually abolished.

Of baptism it may be said that it represents the burial and resurrection of Jesus Christ. This we learn from the following passages: "Know ye not that so many of us as were baptized into Jesus Christ were baptized into his death? Therefore we are buried [Greek, *were buried*] with him by baptism into death; that like as Christ was raised up from the dead by the glory of the Father, even so we also should walk in newness of life. For if we have been planted together in the likeness of his death, we shall be also in the likeness of his resurrection;" "Buried with him in baptism, wherein also ye are risen with him, through the faith of the operation of God, who hath raised him from the dead;" "The like figure whereunto even baptism doth also now save us (not the putting away of the filth of the flesh, but the answer of a good conscience toward God), by the resurrection of Jesus Christ" (Rom. vi. 3, 4, 5; Col. ii. 12; 1 Pet. iii. 21).

It is clear from these passages that baptism has a commemorative reference to the burial and resurrection of Christ. The two ordinances of the gospel symbolically proclaim its three great facts. These facts, as Paul teaches (1 Cor. xv. 3, 4), are that Christ died, was buried, and rose again. The Lord's Supper commemorates the first fact; all are agreed in this view. At his Table the disciples of Christ are solemnly reminded of his death. They weep over him as crucified—dead. In baptism they see him *buried* and *raised again*, just as they see him *dead* in the sacred Supper. Baptism is therefore a symbolic proclamation of two of the three prominent gospel facts—the burial and the resurrection of Christ. These facts are infinitely worthy of commemoration, and they are properly commemorated when the ordinances of the New Testament are observed according to their original design. This by the way.

Baptism also expresses in emblem the believer's death to sin and resurrection to "newness of life." In "repentance toward God and faith toward our Lord Jesus Christ" there occurs a spiritual death to sin, followed by a spiritual resurrection to a new life. These two facts are emblematically set forth in baptism. Hence the absurdity of baptizing any who are not dead to sin. We are baptized into the death of Christ. We profess our reliance on his death for salvation; and we profess also that, as he died *for* sin, we have died *to* sin. As burial is a palpable separation of the dead from the living, so baptism is a symbolic separation of those dead to sin from those living in sin. As a resurrection from the dead indicates an entrance into a new sphere of existence, so baptism, in its similitude to a resurrection, denotes an entrance upon a new life. Dr. Chalmers, therefore, in his lecture on Rom. vi. 3–7, remarks that we "are conceived, in the act of descending under the water of baptism, to have resigned an old life, and in the act of ascending to emerge into a second or new life." There is an emblematic renunciation of "the old life," and there is an emblematic introduction into "the new life." William Tyndale very appropriately says, "The plunging into the water signifieth that we die and are buried with Christ as concerning the old life of sin, which is Adam. And the pulling out again signifieth that we rise again with Christ in a new life, full of the Holy Ghost."

If baptism is a symbol of death to sin, it is of necessity a symbol of regeneration, because death to sin is involved in regeneration. In the words "washing of regeneration" the abstract is probably used for the concrete, the meaning being "the washing of the regenerate." The much-controverted phrase "born of water" seems to refer to baptism. Burial in baptism has respect to *immersion* in water, while "born of water"—literally, "out of water"—has respect to *emersion* out of the watery envelopment which constitutes the symbolic burial. If baptism is a symbol of regeneration, it follows that regeneration must precede it; for otherwise nothing would be symbolized. If, as some suppose, baptism *effects* regeneration, or *is* regeneration, then it cannot be a symbol; for no symbol can produce that which it symbolizes, and no symbol can symbolize itself. In other words, the thing symbolized must have an existence, or there is no place for a symbol. This is plain to those who understand the philosophy of symbols.

Baptism is likewise a symbol of remission of sins, the washing away of sins, and moral purification. We therefore read in Acts ii. 38, "Repent and be baptized, every one of you, in the name of Jesus Christ, for the remission of sins." Many scriptures teach that sins are actually, really, remitted when the sinner believes in Christ; but there is a symbolic, formal, declarative remission in baptism. If sins are remitted when we believe in Christ, and if they are remitted when we are baptized, it is certain that the two remissions are not the same. The one is real, the other is symbolic. In the language addressed to Saul of Tarsus (Acts xxii. 16)—"Arise, and be baptized, and wash away thy sins, calling on the name of the Lord"—there is not so much a contemplation of sins in the light of crimes needing remission as in the aspect of pollutions needing to be washed away. There is an actual washing away of sins in the blood of Christ when faith unites the soul to him; but there is a symbolic washing away of sins in the baptismal waters. When our bodies are said to be washed "with pure water," baptism is referred to as the symbol of moral purification. The symbol has to do with the body, "the outer man," because the soul, "the inner man," has been washed in the blood of Jesus. The outward cleansing follows the inward purification.

Baptism likewise anticipates the believer's resurrection from the dead. This we learn from 1 Cor. xv. 29: "Else what shall they do which are baptized for the dead, if the dead rise not at all? Why are they then baptized for the dead?" These questions are to be found in an argument of matchless power and beauty on the resurrection of the dead. Some of the Corinthians, it seems, denied the doctrine of the resurrection; yet it does not appear that they questioned the propriety of the observance of the ordinance of baptism. Paul virtually tells them that baptism has an anticipatory reference to the resurrection on the last day. It has this reference because it has a commemorative reference to the resurrection of Christ. It anticipates because it commemorates. The reason is obvious. The resurrection of the Lord Jesus procures the resurrection of his followers, and is an infallible pledge of it. The two resurrections are inseparable. Baptism, therefore, while it commemorates the resurrection of Christ, anticipates, of necessity, the resurrection of believers. Dr. Adam Clarke, distinguished among Methodists, in his comment on the verse under consideration, says: "The sum of the apostle's meaning appears to be this: If there be no resurrection of the dead, those who, in becoming Christians, expose themselves to all manner of privations, crosses, severe sufferings, and a violent death, can have no compensation, nor any motive sufficient to induce them to expose themselves to such miseries. But as they receive baptism as an emblem of *death* in voluntarily going under the water, so they receive it as an emblem of the *resurrection* unto eternal *life* in coming up out of the water: thus they are *baptized for the dead,* in perfect faith of the resurrection."

That Dr. Clarke has given the meaning of this controverted passage there is, in my judgment, no ground for reasonable doubt.

Now, if these views of the design and the emblematic import of baptism are correct, it follows inevitably that the immersion in water of a believer in Christ is essential to baptism—so essential that without it there is no baptism. If baptism represents the burial and the resurrection of Christ, it must be immersion. Do the sprinkling and the pouring of water bear any resemblance to a burial and a resurrection? Absolutely none. Immersion, however, bears a striking resemblance to a burial and a resurrection. We are "buried by baptism"—that is, by means of baptism. When the baptismal act is performed, there is a burial. The two things are inseparable, and therefore where there is no "burial" there is no baptism. Were it necessary, I might show that Wall, Whitefield, Wesley, Doddridge, Chalmers, Macknight, Bloomfield, Barnes, and many others—all of them Pedobaptists—admit that the phrase "buried by baptism" alludes to immersion. Some learned men, however, insist that there is no reference to "water baptism." "Spiritual baptism," say they, "is referred to." They think to nullify in this way the argument for immersion. But do they accomplish their object? Let us see. I will meet them on their own chosen ground. Let it be conceded, then, for argument's sake, that "buried by baptism" denotes spiritual baptism. Then there is a spiritual burial. Now, it is a well-settled point among Pedobaptists that the outward baptism is a sign of the inward. If, then, the inward baptism involves a spiritual burial, the outward baptism must involve a burial in water that it may represent the inward. Men may torture and put to the rack the phrase "buried by baptism," but it will testify of immersion. It cannot be divested of its reference to Christian immersion.

To conclude the argument from the design of baptism: How stands the matter? If baptism commemorates the burial and the resurrection of Christ, it must be immersion. If it is an emblematic representation of death to sin and resurrection to newness of life, the representation is essentially incomplete without immersion. If it symbolizes the remission of sins, the washing away of sins, and moral purification, the purposes of the symbol require immersion. The fulness of the remission, the thoroughness of the washing, and the completeness of the purification demand an act affecting the whole body. If there is something in baptism that anticipates and resembles the resurrection of the dead, still it must be immersion. Sprinkling and pouring are as unlike a resurrection as they are unlike a burial.

Let baptism be considered a representation of the facts illustrated in the design of the ordinance, and it will appear not only an impressive symbol, but a combination of symbols as beautiful as they are solemn. If another form of expression is preferred, it may be said that kindred elements come together and constitute the symbol. In immersion alone is there a recognition of these elements, and therefore immersion alone is the symbol. No act but *immersion in water,* followed by *emersion out of water,* meets the demands of the symbol. Any other act vitiates the symbolic import of baptism.

SECTION V.

The places selected for the administration of baptism and the circumstances attending its administration, as referred to in the New Testament, supply an additional argument in proof of the position of Baptists.

John baptized in Jordan. That the Jordan is a suitable stream for purposes of immersion is manifest from the testimony of one of the most distinguished of modern travellers and scholars, Dr. Edward Robinson.

Speaking of the Jordan, he says, "We estimated the breadth of the stream to be from eighty to one hundred feet. The guides supposed it to be now ten or twelve feet deep. I bathed in the river without going out into the deep channel."*

Even Dr. Lightfoot, who was quite conspicuous in his opposition to immersion in the Westminster Assembly, uses the following language: "That the baptism of John was by plunging the body seems to appear from those things which are related of him—namely, that he *baptized in Jordan;* that he baptized in *Enon, because there was much water there;* and that Christ, being baptized, *came up out of the water;* to which that seems to be parallel (Acts viii. 38), '*Philip and the eunuch went down into the water.*'" †

I am aware that Pedobaptists—many of them, at least—argue that John's was not Christian baptism, that he did not live under the Christian Dispensation, etc. Dissenting most earnestly from these views, I waive a consideration of them as foreign to my present purpose. It is sufficient for me to say that even if it could be shown that John's was not Christian baptism it would avail Pedobaptists nothing. John performed an act called baptism, and various circumstances, as well as the meaning of the word, indicate that that act

---

* *Biblical Researches in Palestine,* vol. ii., p. 256.

† Quoted in Dr. Adam Clarke's *Commentary,* vol. v., p. 325.

was immersion. Pedobaptists attempt to invalidate the force of those circumstances by denying that John administered *Christian* baptism. But they admit that the apostles, after the resurrection of Christ, administered Christian baptism. Very well. The same term used to designate the act performed by John is used to denote the act performed by them. It must therefore be the same act. Surely, no one will say that the word "baptize" means one thing in its connection with John's ministry and a different thing in connection with the ministry of the apostles. Hence I repeat that if it could be shown that John's was not Christian baptism it would amount to nothing.

There is another Pedobaptist view which requires notice. It is that Christ was baptized to initiate him into the priestly office. A few questions will place this matter in its proper light: Was not Christ "made a priest after the order of Melchisedec, and not after the order of Aaron"? How could he be a priest according to the law of Moses, when he was of the "tribe of Judah"? Was not the priestly office confined to the tribe of Levi, and to the family of Aaron in that tribe? Did not the law say, "The stranger that cometh nigh shall be put to death"? All that Pedobaptists say about the baptismal initiation of Christ into the priestly office is at war with the Scriptures. Why this attempt to show that the Saviour was made a priest by his baptism? The object seems to be to evade the moral power of his example; for no man who will lay aside his prejudices can deny that Jesus was immersed in the Jordan. But if the people can be made to believe that the baptism of Christ had reference to his priestly consecration, they will feel comparatively exempt from obligation to follow his example, as they are not baptized that they may become priests. Jesus, in his baptism as well as in other respects, has "left us an example that we should follow his steps."

Returning from this apparent digression, I may say again that the Jordan was unquestionably a suitable stream for purposes of immersion; that John baptized in it; and that Jesus, when baptized, "went up straightway out of the water." John also baptized "in Enon near to Salim" (John iii. 23). Why? Let Dr. Miller answer. He says: "Independently of immersion altogether, plentiful streams of water were absolutely necessary for the constant refreshment and sustenance of the many thousands who were encamped from day to day to witness the preaching and the baptism of this extraordinary man; together with the beasts employed for their transportation. Only figure to yourselves a large encampment of men, women, and children, etc. . . . As a poor man who lived in the wilderness, whose raiment was of the meanest kind, and whose food was such alone as the desert afforded, it is not to be supposed that he possessed appropriate vessels for administering baptism to multitudes by pouring or sprinkling. He therefore seems to have made use of the neighboring stream of water for this purpose, descending its banks and setting his feet on its margin, so as to admit of his using a handful to answer the symbolic purpose intended by the application of water in baptism." *

What to call this extract I do not know. It seems to be a mixture of assertion, supposition, and fiction. Where did Dr. Miller learn that "plentiful streams of water were absolutely necessary" for the purposes which he specifies? What he says about "a large encampment" must have been a day-dream, as also his reference to "beasts" and "transportation." The evangelists say nothing of the "encampment" and make no allusion to the "beasts." Poverty is an inconvenience, but not a crime; and I therefore take no offence at the reference to the indigence of the first Baptist preacher. It may, however, be questioned whether John was not able to own "appropriate vessels" for purposes of "pouring or sprinkling." But, admitting his extreme poverty when he went to the Jordan to baptize, he then became so popular that an intimation from him that he needed "appropriate

* Miller *On Baptism: Four Discourses*, pp. 92, 93.

126   *DISTINCTIVE PRINCIPLES OF BAPTISTS.*

vessels" would have secured as many as the "beasts" could transport. Why did he not, then, get "vessels" and supersede the necessity of his going to the Jordan, and to "Enon near to Salim, because there was much water there"? Would not Herod also have furnished "appropriate vessels" at the time when he "did many things, and heard John gladly"?

Dr. N. L. Rice, having been a pupil of Dr. Miller, adopted his view of the matter before us. He therefore, in his *Debate with Alexander Campbell* (p. 193), uses these words: "John, it is true, was baptizing in Enon near Salim, because there was much water there. But did he want much water to baptize in, or did he want it for other purposes? As I have already stated, multitudes of the Jews who resorted to him remained together several days at a time. They must observe their daily ablutions. For these and for ordinary purposes they needed much water; but it cannot be proved that John wanted the water for the purpose of baptizing."

Theologians should, of course, be wise men, but they ought not to be "wise above that which is written." Where did Dr. Rice learn that the "multitudes" who went to John "remained together several days"? Who told him about those "daily ablutions"? By what sort of logic can it be shown that the Jews "needed much water" for other purposes, but not for baptismal purposes, when baptism is the only thing requiring water mentioned in the controverted passage?

It is humiliating to know that such men as Drs. Miller and Rice have used the language that has been quoted. Let modern teachers now keep silence, and let an evangelist speak. What does he say? Here are his inspired words: "And John also was *baptizing* in Enon near to Salim, because there was much water there: and they came, and were baptized" (John iii. 23). Is there anything here about "encampments," "beasts," "daily ablutions," etc.? Did not the people go to John to be *baptized?*—not to encamp, not to provide water for their "beasts," not to "observe their daily ablutions." Did not John select Enon as a suitable place for his purpose "because there was much water there"? Did he not need "much water" in baptizing? and is not this a strong argument in favor of immersion? No act performed on the body requires so "much water" as the act of immersing in water. I write in plainness and in sorrow when I say that those who expound the passage under consideration as Drs. Miller and Rice have done assign a reason for John's selection of Enon as a baptismal place which the Holy Spirit has not assigned. The doing of such a thing involves fearful responsibility.

To demolish all that has ever been said about John's

selecting places where there was "much water" for other than baptismal purposes, I need only state a few facts. We are told that in the early part of the Saviour's ministry "great multitudes followed him;" subsequently, he miraculously fed "four thousand," and at another time "five thousand men, besides women and children;" and on another occasion "there were gathered together an innumerable multitude of people, insomuch that they trod one upon another." But there was nothing said about water. It is not said that Jesus, "seeing the multitudes," went where there was "much water," that the people might be refreshed, but "he went up into a mountain." Was he less considerate than was John of the comfort of the crowds that attended him? We cannot believe it. Still, there is nothing said about "much water" in connection with the multitudes that gathered around him. But we are told of "much water" in the account given of John's baptism in Enon. He "was baptizing in Enon near to Salim, because there was much water there." It is vain, and worse than vain, to deny that "much water" was required in baptism. This would not have been the case if baptism had not been immersion. Of the many acts popularly called baptism, there is only one—the act of immersion—that requires "much water;" and it is certain that this is the act performed by John the Baptist.

DISTINCTIVE PRINCIPLES OF BAPTISTS. 129

The baptism of the Ethiopian eunuch, as recorded in Acts viii. 38, 39, is worthy of special notice. The sacred historian says, "And they went down both into the water, both Philip and the eunuch; and he baptized him;" "And when they were come up out of the water," etc. It has been often said that going into the water does not *necessarily* imply immersion. This is true. It is possible to go "down into water" and "come up out of water" without being immersed. But suppose, as in the case before us, between the two movements the act of baptism occurs. What then? Evidently the word "baptize" must determine the nature of that act. This is the view held by Baptists. They say, with strongest emphasis, that the term "baptize" shows what act Philip performed after he went down with the eunuch into the water; and they confidently appeal to all Greek literature, secular and sacred, in support of the position that *baptizo* means "to immerse." Hence they would be as fully satisfied as they now are of the eunuch's immersion if not one word had been said about the descent into the water. Still, they regard the going down into the water and the coming up out of the water as furnishing a very strong circumstantial proof of immersion. They assume that Philip and the eunuch were men of good sense, and therefore did not go into the water for purposes of "pouring or sprinkling."

130   DISTINCTIVE PRINCIPLES OF BAPTISTS.

But it is often said that the Greek preposition *eis*, translated "into," means "to," and that Philip and the eunuch went only *to* the water. As sensible men they would not have done this if sprinkling or pouring had been the act to be performed.

With reference to this little word *eis*, Dr. Summers, in his book *On Baptism* (p. 100), says: "When *eis* means 'into,' it is used before the noun as well as before the verb." The argument based on this statement is that, as *eis* is used but once in Acts viii. 38, Philip and the eunuch did not go *into*, but only *to*, the water; and the conclusion is that "the eunuch was not immersed."

I concede everything which truth requires me to concede to Dr. Summers. It is true that when entrance into a place or thing is denoted *eis* is frequently used twice—once in composition with the verb, and once before the noun or pronoun; but in numberless instances it is used but once to express the same idea of entrance. Let any Greek scholar turn to Matt. ii. 11–14, 20–22, and he will find *eis* but once in the phrases "into the house," "into their own country," "into Egypt," "into the land of Israel," and "into the parts of Galilee." If, then, Dr. Summers's statement is true without qualification, the "wise men" did not go "*into* the house" and did not return "*into* their own country," nor was Joseph required to "flee *into* Egypt" and to "go *into* the land of Israel."

Again, if Dr. Summers is right in his assertion, the demons referred to in Matt. viii. 31–33 did not enter "*into* the swine," and the swine did not run "*into* the sea," and the keepers of the swine did not go "*into* the city." In all these places *eis* is used but once. It seems, also, that the Saviour, in Matt. ix. 17, did not speak of putting wine *into* bottles, but only *to* bottles; for *eis* is used but once. Query: How could the "new wine" break the "old bottles" without being put into them? Once more: It is said in Matt. xxv. 46, "And these shall go away *into* everlasting punishment, but the righteous *into* life eternal." Here, also, *eis* is used but once; and, according to Dr. Summers and many others, the wicked do not go "*into* everlasting punishment" nor the righteous "*into* life eternal." But in these passages Pedobaptists very readily admit that *eis* means "into." They have no objection to this meaning unless baptismal waters are referred to.

This little word *eis* is a strange word indeed if all said of it is true. It will take a man *into* a country, *into* a city, *into* a house, *into* a ship, *into* heaven, *into* hell—*into* any place in the universe except the water. Poor word! Afflicted, it seems, with hydrophobia, it will allow a person to go *to* the water, but not *into* it. However, where baptism is not referred to, it may denote entrance into water, as in Mark ix. 22: "And ofttimes it hath cast him into the fire and into the waters to destroy him." Unfortunate boy! that *eis*, though used but once, thrust him "into the fire and into the waters."

Pedobaptists are very unreasonable in their management of the baptismal controversy. They insist that it is utterly improbable that water could be found in Jerusalem for the immersion of three thousand persons on the day of Pentecost—that there is no mention of a stream of water in connection with the baptism of Saul of Tarsus and the jailer. One would imagine that if there was anything said about "a river," "much water," something would be at once conceded in favor of immersion. But not so. For when Baptists refer to the Jordan or Enon, where there was "much water," or to the water into which Philip and the eunuch went down, Pedobaptists argue that an abundance of water by no means indicates that the act of immersion was performed. We cannot please them at all. They are like the Jewish children in the market-places. If we pipe to them, they will not dance; if we mourn to them, they will not lament. If there is no mention of a "river" in a baptismal narrative of the New Testament, the cry is, "No immersion" and "Scarcity of water." If the river Jordan is named, the same cry of "No immersion" is heard; so that, according to Pedobaptist logic, scarcity of water and abundance of water prove the same thing! How are we to meet in argument men who draw the same conclusion from premises as far apart as "from the centre thrice to the utmost pole"?

John Calvin felt the force of the argument in favor of immersion derived from the places selected for the administration of baptism. Hence, in his commentary (translated by Rev. William Pringle, Edinburgh, and printed for the Calvin Translation Society), he remarks on John iii. 22, 23: "From these words we may infer that John and Christ administered baptism by plunging the whole body beneath the water." On Acts viii. 38 he says: "Here we see the rite used among the men of old time in baptism; for they put all the body into the water. Now, the use is this, that the minister doth only sprinkle the body or the head. But we ought not to stand so much about a small difference of a ceremony that we should therefore divide the church or trouble the same with brawls. . . . Wherefore the church did grant liberty to herself since the beginning to change the rites somewhat, excepting the substance." So much for the testimony of the great Calvin.

Before proceeding to the historical argument for immersion, I will say that if *baptizo* means "to immerse," it does not mean "sprinkle" or "pour." If it means "sprinkle," it does not mean "immerse" or "pour." If it means "pour," it does not mean "sprinkle" or "immerse." It is at war with the philosophy of language to say that the word can denote three acts so dissimilar. Did not Jesus Christ, in enjoining baptism, give a specific command? If he did not, it is impossible to know what he requires, and the impossibility releases from all obligation to obey the requirement. I say boldly that it is not the duty of any man to be baptized if he *cannot* know what baptism is. All candid persons must admit that the Saviour gave a specific command when he enjoined baptism on believers. If so, he did not require them to be immersed in water, *or* that water be sprinkled *or* poured on them. He did not require any *one* of three things; for on this supposition the command loses its specific character. The matter, then, comes to this point: Did Christ require believers to be immersed in water, or to have water applied to them by sprinkling or pouring?

Now, if the word "baptize" in the New Testament means "sprinkle" or "pour," as Pedobaptists insist, and if baptism is an "application of water," is it not very remarkable that water is never said to be baptized upon the subjects of the ordinance, and never said to be applied? If "baptize" means "to sprinkle" or "pour," the water is baptized, not the person.

We cannot speak of sprinkling a man without an ellipsis or figure of speech; and no one would expect an ellipsis or figure of speech in the Apostolic Commission. Sprinkling implies the separation and scattering of the particles of the substance sprinkled. A man cannot be poured, because pouring implies a continuous stream of the substance poured. I say, again, that if "baptize" in the New Testament means "sprinkle" or "pour," the water is baptized. But nowhere is water found in the objective case after the verb "baptize" in the active voice, and nowhere is it the subject of the verb in the passive voice. We never read, " I baptize *water* upon you," but, "I baptize *you*." It is never said that water *was baptized* upon them, but it is said that "they *were baptized*, both men and women." The subjects of the ordinance are baptized, the water is not; and therefore "baptize" in the New Testament signifies neither "sprinkle" nor "pour." But substitute "immerse" for it, and how plain and beautiful is every baptismal narrative! I immerse *you*, not the water. *They* were immersed—that is, the "*men and women*." The plainness of this view renders a further elucidation of the point needless.

SECTION VI.

History bears testimony to the practice of immersion, except in cases of sickness and urgent necessity, for more than thirteen hundred years.

I avail myself, as I have already done, of Pedobaptist witnesses. My first witness is Richard Baxter, author of the *Saint's Rest*. He says, "It is commonly confessed by us to the Anabaptists, as our commentators declare, that in the apostles' times the baptized were dipped over head in the water, and that this signified their profession both of believing the burial and resurrection of Christ, and of their own *present* renouncing the world and flesh, or dying to sin and living to Christ, or rising again to newness of life, or being buried and risen again with Christ, as the apostle expoundeth in the forecited texts of Col. ii. and Rom. vi." *

The celebrated Dr. Samuel Johnson refers to the Roman Catholics as in the Lord's Supper giving the bread to the laity and withholding the cup from them. He says, "They may think that in what is merely ritual, deviations from the primitive mode may be admitted on the ground of convenience; and I think they are as well warranted to make this alteration as we are to substitute sprinkling in the room of the ancient baptism." †

John Wesley, in his *Journal* of Feb. 21, 1736, writes as follows: "Mary Welsh, aged eleven days, was baptized, according to the custom of the first church and the rule of the Church of England, by immersion."

* Quoted in Booth's *Pedobaptism Examined*.
† Boswell's *Life of Johnson*, vol. ii., p. 383.

Dr. Miller, with his bitter opposition to immersion, says: "It is not denied that for the first few centuries after Christ the most common mode of administering baptism was by immersion."*

The learned Mosheim, in his *Church History*, says of the first century: "The sacrament of *baptism* was administered in this century, without the public assemblies, in places appointed and prepared for that purpose, and was performed by an immersion of the whole body in the baptismal font." Of the second century he says: "The persons that were to be baptized, after they had repeated the Creed, confessed and renounced their sins, and particularly the devil and his pompous allurements, were immersed under water and received into Christ's kingdom." Of the fourth century he writes thus: "Baptismal fonts were now erected in the porch of each church, for the more commodious administration of that initiating sacrament." †

The celebrated church historian Neander, in his letter to Rev. Willard Judd, expresses himself thus: "As to your question on the original rite of baptism, there can be no doubt whatever that in the primitive times the ceremony was performed by immersion, to signify a complete immersion into the new principle of life divine which was to be imparted by the Mes-

---

* *Sermons on Baptism*, p. 116.

† Maclaine's *Mosheim* (in two vols.), vol. i., pp. 46, 69, 121.

siah. When St. Paul says that through baptism we are buried with Christ, and rise again with him, he unquestionably alludes to the symbol of dipping into, and rising again out of, the water. The practice of immersion in the first centuries was beyond all doubt prevalent in the whole church; the only exception was made with the baptism of the sick, hence termed *baptisma clinicorum*, which was performed merely by sprinkling."* I might quote other testimony like this from Neander's *Church History* and his *Planting and Training of the Christian Church*, but the foregoing from the great Lutheran is sufficient.

Dr. Whitby of the Church of England, in his commentary, says on Rom. vi. 4, "It being so expressly declared here and in Col. ii. 12 that we are 'buried with Christ in baptism' by being buried under water, and the argument to oblige us to a conformity to his death by dying to sin being taken hence, and this immersion being religiously observed by all Christians for thirteen centuries, and approved by our church, and the change of it into sprinkling, even without any allowance from the Author of the institution, or any license from any Council of the church, being that which the Romanist still urgeth to justify his refusal of the cup to the laity,—it were to be wished that this custom might be again of general use, and aspersion

* See Appendix to Judd's *Review of Stuart*.

only permitted, as of old, in case of *clinici* or those in present danger of death."

What says Professor Stuart? Quoting Augusti, who refers to the ancient practice of immersion as "a thing made out," he says: "So, indeed, all the writers who have thoroughly investigated this subject conclude. I know of no one usage of ancient times which seems to be more clearly and certainly made out. I cannot see how it is possible for any candid man who examines the subject to deny this." Again: "The mode of baptism by immersion the Oriental Church has always continued to preserve, even down to the present time. The members of this church are accustomed to call the members of the Western churches *sprinkled Christians*, by way of ridicule and contempt. They maintain that *baptizo* can mean nothing but 'immerge,' and that 'baptism by sprinkling' is as great a solecism as 'immersion by aspersion;' and they claim to themselves the honor of having preserved the ancient sacred rite of the church free from change and corruption which would destroy its significancy." *

As immersion was the general practice for more than thirteen hundred years, the reader may wish to know how it has been to so lamentable an extent superseded by sprinkling. The following quotations explain the matter.

* Stuart *On the Mode of Baptism*, pp. 75–77.

Dr. Wall, in his *History of Infant Baptism*, speaking of the reign of Queen Elizabeth, which continued from A. D. 1558 to 1603, says: "It being allowed to weak children (tho' strong enough to be brought to church) to be baptized by affusion, many fond ladies and gentlewomen first, and then by degrees the common people, would obtain the favor of the priest to have their children pass for weak children too tender to endure dipping in water. Especially (as Mr. Walker observes) *if some instance really were, or were but fancied or framed, of some child's taking hurt by it.* And another thing that had a greater influence than this was: That many of our *English* divines and other people had, during Queen Mary's bloody reign, fled into Germany, Switzerland, etc., and, coming back in Queen Elizabeth's time, they brought with them a great love to the customs of those Protestant churches wherein they had sojourned. And especially the authority of *Calvin*, and the rules which he had established at Geneva, had a mighty influence on a great number of our people about that time. Now, *Calvin* had not only given his Dictate, in his Institutions, that *the difference is of no moment, whether he that is baptized be dipt all over; and if so, whether thrice or once; or whether he be only wetted with the water poured on him:* But he had also drawn up for the use of his church at *Geneva* (and afterward published to the world) *a form of administering the sacraments,* where, when he comes to the order of baptizing, he words it thus: *Then the minister of baptism pours water on the infant; saying, I baptize thee,* etc. There had been, as I said, some Synods in some Dioceses of *France* that had spoken of affusion without mentioning immersion at all; that being the common practice: but for an Office or Liturgy of any church; this is, I believe the first in the world that prescribes affusion absolutely."

Dr. Wall also refers to the influence of the Westminster Assembly in substituting pouring and sprinkling for immersion. That Assembly not only made a "Confession of Faith," but a "Directory for the Public Worship of God," in which "pouring or sprinkling" is declared "not only lawful, but sufficient and most expedient." Such a declaration surely would not have been made if "pouring" and "sprinkling" had not been of comparatively recent origin in England. This, however, by way of parenthesis. Dr. Wall says: "So (parallel to the rest of their reformations) they reformed the Font into a Basin. This Learned Assembly could not remember that Fonts to baptize in had been always used by the primitive Christians, long before the beginning of popery; and ever since churches were built: But that sprinkling, for the common use of baptizing, was really introduced (in *France* first, and then in other Popish countries) in times of Popery: And that accordingly all those countries in which the usurped power of the Pope is, or has formerly been, owned have left off dipping of children in the Font: But that all other countries in the world (which had never regarded his authority) do still use it: And that Basins, except in case of necessity, were never used by Papists, or any other Christians whatsoever, till by themselves. The use was: The minister continuing in his reading Desk, the child was brought and held below him: And there was placed for that use a little Basin of water about the bigness of a syllabub pot, into which the minister dipping his fingers, and then holding his hand over the face of the child, some drops would fall from his fingers on the child's face. For the *Directory* says, it is *not only lawful, but most expedient,* to use pouring or sprinkling." *

I quote also, in vindication of the "truth of history," from the *Edinburgh Encyclopædia,* edited by Sir David Brewster, a very distinguished Pedobaptist. It contains the following account of "sprinkling:" "The first law for sprinkling was obtained in the following manner: Pope Stephen II., being driven from Rome by Astolphus, King of the Lombards, in 753, fled to Pepin, who a short time before had usurped the crown of France. While he remained

---

* *History of Infant Baptism,* part ii., chap. ix.

there the monks of Cressy, in Brittany, consulted him whether in case of necessity baptism performed by pouring water on the head of the infant would be lawful. Stephen replied that it would. But though the truth of this fact should be allowed—which, however, some Catholics deny—yet pouring or sprinkling was admitted only in cases of necessity. It was not till the year 1311 that the legislature, in a Council held at Ravenna, declared immersion or sprinkling to be indifferent. In this country [Scotland], however, sprinkling was never practised in ordinary cases till after the Reformation; and in England, even in the reign of Edward VI., trine immersion was commonly observed. But during the persecution of Mary many persons, most of whom were Scotsmen, fled from England to Geneva, and there greedily imbibed the opinions of that church. In 1556 a book was published at that place containing 'The Form of Prayers and Ministration of Sacraments, approved by the famous and godly learned man, John Calvin,' in which the administrator is enjoined to take water in his hand and lay it on the child's forehead. These Scottish exiles, who had renounced the authority of the Pope, implicitly acknowledged the authority of Calvin, and, returning to their own country, with John Knox at their head, in 1559, established sprinkling in Scotland. From Scotland this practice made its way into England in the reign of Elizabeth, but was not authorized by the Established Church." *

My last quotation bearing on the history of baptism I make from Dean Stanley of the Church of England. In his article on "Baptism" in the *Nineteenth Century* for October, 1879, in referring to immersion, he says: "Even in the Church of England it is still observed in theory. Elizabeth and Edward VI. were both immersed. The rubric in the Public Baptism for Infants enjoins that, unless for special cases, they are to be dipped, not sprinkled. But in practice it gave way since the beginning of the seventeenth century. . . . The reason of the change is obvious. The practice of immersion, apostolic and primitive as it was, was peculiarly suitable to the southern and eastern countries, for which it was designed, and peculiarly unsuitable to the tastes, the convenience, and the feelings of the countries of the North and West. Not by any decree of Council or Parliament, but by the general sentiment of Christian liberty, this great change was effected. Not beginning till the thirteenth century, it has gradually driven the ancient Catholic usage out of the whole of Europe. There is no one who would now wish to go back to the old practice. It had, no doubt, the sanction of the

* Article "Baptism."

apostles and of their Master. It had the sanction of the venerable churches of the early ages and of the sacred countries of the East. Baptism by sprinkling was rejected by the whole ancient church (except in the rare case of deathbeds or extreme necessity) as no baptism at all."

In speaking of the decision of "the Christian civilized world" against immersion, he says: "It is a striking example of the triumph of common sense and convenience over the bondage of form and custom. Perhaps no greater change has ever taken place in the outward form of Christian ceremony with such general agreement. It is a greater change even than that which the Roman Catholic Church has made in administering the sacrament of the Lord's Supper in the bread without the wine. For that was a change which did not affect the thing that was signified; whereas the change from immersion to sprinkling has set aside the larger part of the apostolic language regarding baptism, and has altered the very meaning of the word."

Dean Stanley's testimony to historical facts can be safely accepted; but when he said that the change of immersion into sprinkling was a "triumph of common sense and convenience," his language can be accounted for in one way: he was what is termed a "Broad Churchman," and his views were quite elastic. There is no very great difference between a German Rationalist and an English Broad Churchman. It would be out of place now for me to enter into a descriptive detail of the opinions of either.

If I have not proved that immersion was practised for more than thirteen hundred years, except in cases of sickness and urgent necessity, I may well despair of proving anything. He who is not convinced by the testimony adduced in support of this fact would not be "persuaded though one should rise from the dead." What, then, is to be said of those Pedobaptists who assert that "it cannot be proved that immersion was practised before the sixteenth century"? They should study church history, and from it they would learn that until the last few hundred years immersion was the general rule, and aspersion the exception. They would learn that at one period the validity of a copious pouring of water on the entire persons of the sick on their beds, instead of baptism, was seriously called in question, and by some positively denied. They would ascertain that many more *infants* had been immersed in water than ever had water sprinkled or poured on them. The man who denies this fact knows very little about ecclesiastical history. Immersion, however, so far as infants are concerned, is no better than sprinkling. Neither is commanded in the word of God, and both belong to the large family of human traditions.

SECTION VII.
Pedobaptist objections answered.

These are numerous, and all of them cannot be referred to in a book like this. I will, however, refer to the most prominent objections that have come to my notice. They are the following:

1. *It is said that John baptized, not in, but at, Jordan.*

Episcopalians and Methodists are precluded from a resort to this objection, for the "Book of Common Prayer" and the "Discipline" both teach that Jesus was baptized "*in* the Jordan." In all the range of Greek literature the preposition *en*, used in Matt. iii. 6, and translated "in" means "in." Harrison, who is high authority on "Greek prepositions," refers to it as "the same with the Latin and English 'in'" (p. 243). It is a suggestive fact that our "in" comes to us through the Latin tongue from the Greek *en*. A child at a very early age learns what "in" means. To make the point before us plain it needs only to be said that John "baptized *in* the wilderness." Here we have the same "in" representing the Greek *en*. How would it do to say that John baptized *at* the wilderness? The Greek is surely a strange language if it has no preposition meaning "in;" and if *en* has not this meaning, there is no word in the language that has. Let any Greek scholar try to express in Greek the idea of being *in* a place, *in* a house, or *in* a river without the use of *en*. The meaning of *en* is "in," as that of *eis* is "into;" and therefore it follows that John baptized *in* the Jordan, not *at* it.

2. *John, it is said, baptized "with water."*

It is insisted that "with water" implies that the water was applied in baptism. It is enough to say, in answer to this objection, that Baptists never immerse *without* water. John speaks of baptism *in* water, *in* the Holy Spirit, and *in* fire. King James's translators probably rendered *en* "with" to make what they thought an emphatic distinction between the baptismal elements. They were wrong. Every scholar knows that the proper rendering is "in water." The little preposition *en* here also acts a conspicuous part. It is as proper to say that John baptized *with* the wilderness and *with* the Jordan as that he baptized *with* water. In the first two instances *en* is translated "in," and why should it be rendered "with" in the last? But, as I have said, Baptists do not immerse without water. If it is affirmed that the clothes were washed *with* water, does it follow that they were not dipped *into* it? Surely not.

3. *It is urged with great confidence that three thousand persons could not have been immersed on the day of Pentecost.*

It is supposed that there was not sufficient water for the purpose. Indeed! Where now is the "much water" that Dr. Rice found necessary for the "daily ablutions" of the Jews? They certainly performed their "ablutions" at home if they could not be dispensed with when they went to John's baptism. Jerusalem, according to Dr. Edward Robinson, "would appear always to have had a full supply of water for its inhabitants, both in ancient and modern times. In the numerous sieges to which, in all ages, it has been exposed, we nowhere read of any want of water within the city."*

Where people can live, there is sufficient water for purposes of immersion. But why dwell on this point? If Jerusalem had been situated on the Mediterranean Sea, many Pedobaptists would not permit *eis* to take the three thousand converts *into* its waters. They are no more willing to admit immersion where there is an abundance of water than where there is a supposed scarcity.

But it is insisted that it was impossible, even if there was water enough, for three thousand to be immersed in one day, and that therefore water must have been sprinkled or poured on them. I answer that it takes about as much time to sprinkle or pour as to immerse. Much the greater portion of time, in modern baptisms,

* *Biblical Researches in Palestine*, vol. i., p. 479.

is occupied in repeating the words of the baptismal ceremony. If it is said that sprinkling or pouring was more expeditiously performed in ancient than in modern times, I have an equal right to say the same thing of immersion. If the apostles alone baptized on the day of Pentecost (which, however, cannot be proved), they could have immersed the three thousand. If Pedobaptists deny this, let them account for the historical fact that Austin, the monk sent by Pope Gregory the Great into England in the year 597, "consecrated the river Swale, near York, in which he caused ten thousand of his converts to be baptized in one day." They were immersed.

4. *It is thought to militate against immersion that the Holy Spirit is said to be poured out.*

If so, it militates equally against sprinkling. If pouring is baptism, why is not the Spirit sometimes said to be baptized? He is said to be poured out. There is as much difference between the pouring out of the Spirit and baptism in the Spirit as there is between the pouring of water into a baptistery and the immersion of a person in that water. Those baptized "with the Holy Spirit"—or, rather, "*in* the Holy Spirit"—are placed under the influence of the Spirit, just as a person baptized in water is put under the influence of the water. It is the prerogative of Christ to baptize in the Holy Spirit. If, as Pedobap-

DISTINCTIVE PRINCIPLES OF BAPTISTS. 151

tists insist, pouring is baptism because the Holy Spirit is said to be poured out, what follows? Why, that as the Spirit is said to be "given," to "testify," to "fill," and to "speak," therefore giving, testifying, filling, speaking, are all baptism! This, surely, will not be claimed.

5. *Saul of Tarsus, it is affirmed, was baptized standing up.*

The argument assumes that when it is said (Acts ix. 18) that Saul "arose and was baptized," the meaning is he "stood up and was baptized." In the Greek the participle *anastas* is used, and it comes from a verb found in the New Testament more than a hundred times, rendered in a few places "stood up," and in a hundred places "rise," "arise," or "raise." Wherever "stood up" is found, "arose" would be just as good a translation. Let it be admitted, however, that the word is properly rendered "stand up" in certain passages; still, it is undeniable that it is used in other passages to denote the beginning of a process by which a thing is done. Two examples will be sufficient. It is said (Luke i. 39), "And Mary arose [*anastasa*, same word with a feminine termination] in those days, and went into the hill-country," etc. Did Mary *stand up* and go? Does not *anastasa* here indicate the beginning of the movement by which she reached "the hill-country"? In Luke xv. 18 the prodigal son says,

"I will arise [*anastas*] and go to my father;" and in verse 20 it is said "And he arose [*anastas*] and came to his father." Did he stand up and go to his father? Was not the *anastas* the commencement of the returning movement? He arose and returned to his father. Now, Luke wrote the Acts of the Apostles. Is it not reasonable, then, to believe that when he says (Acts ix. 18) that Saul "arose [*anastas*] and was baptized," he means by *anastas* the beginning of a process necessary to his baptism? He evidently arose that he might be immersed; but no rising up, no *anastas*, was necessary if water was to be poured or sprinkled on him. His immersion implied the movement indicated by *anastas*, while pouring or sprinkling could imply no such movement. In verse 39 of the same chapter it is said, "And Peter arose [*anastas*] and went with them"—that is, to Joppa. He did not stand still and go, but he arose as the first thing to be done in getting to Joppa—just as Saul arose as the first thing to be done in getting to a suitable place for immersion. But I shall let Saul, who afterward became Paul, settle this matter himself. In Rom. vi. 4, including himself with those to whom he wrote, he says: "We are [were] buried with him by baptism." If Saul was buried by baptism, he was immersed. There is no burial in pouring or sprinkling.

6. *It is argued that the question* (Acts x. 47), "*Can*

DISTINCTIVE PRINCIPLES OF BAPTISTS. 153

any man forbid water that these should not be baptized?" intimates that water was to be brought.

This objection to immersion is specially destitute of force. The question only means, Can any one forbid the baptism of these Gentiles, who have received the Holy Spirit as well as the Jews? Baptist ministers, in receiving candidates for baptism, often say to the church, "Can any man forbid water, that these should not be baptized?" Does this imply that the water is to be brought in a "bowl" or a "pitcher"? Evidently not.

7. *It is supposed that the jailer* (Acts xvi. 30-34) *could not have been immersed in prison.*

Baptists do not say that he was immersed in prison. The jailer brought out Paul and Silas from the prison before he said, "Sirs, what must I do to be saved?" Then they "spoke to him the word of the Lord, and to all that were in his house." It seems, then, that they were in his house (verse 32). In verse 34 it is said, "And when he had brought them into his house," etc. Verse 33 contains an account of the baptism. They left the house when the baptism took place, and they went back into the house when the baptism was over. Did they leave the house that the jailer and his family might have water poured or sprinkled on them? Was it necessary? Certainly not, but it was necessary to the administration of apostolic baptism.

8. *Pedobaptists urge that the baptism of the Israelites unto Moses in the cloud and in the sea is irreconcilable with the idea of immersion.*

In being baptized into or unto Christ we publicly assume him as our leader. The Israelites in being baptized unto Moses publicly assumed him as their leader. The resemblance of their passage through the sea, with the cloud above them, to Christian immersion no doubt suggested to Paul the language he employed. There was no literal baptism, and there was no pouring or sprinkling. How often is Ps. lxxvii. 17 referred to to prove that the Israelites had water poured on them! Unfortunately for this view of the matter, it is said, "The *clouds* poured out water." It was a *cloud* that Paul refers to—the miraculous cloud, the symbol of the Divine Presence. This cloud had no more water in it than that on which the Saviour rode triumphantly to heaven. It will be observed that the Israelites were baptized *in the cloud and in the sea.* In literal baptism the water constitutes the envelopment. The person is baptized in water only. In the case of the Israelites it required the sea (which was as a wall on each side) and the cloud (which was above) to complete the envelopment. Who does not see that the word "baptize" is used in connection with the passage of the Israelites through the sea because it means "to immerse"? If it could be conceived that the miraculous cloud poured forth water, and that the pouring constituted the baptism, what had the sea to do in the baptismal operation? Absolutely nothing; but Paul says that "our fathers were . . . baptized unto Moses in the cloud and in the sea" (1 Cor. x. 2).

9. *It is contended that the phrase " divers washings " in Heb. ix. 10 (in the original, " baptisms ") indicates more baptisms than one.*

It is a significant fact that Dr. Macknight, a Presbyterian translator, renders the phrase " divers immersions." The Mosaic law required unclean persons to " bathe themselves in water ;" it required unclean vessels to be " put into water ;" and it said, "All that abideth not the fire ye shall make go through the water " (Num. xxxi. 23). It surely will be conceded that these regulations involved " divers immersions." There were " divers " occasions for immersing, and " divers " objects were immersed. Moreover, in the same chapter of Hebrews the verb *rantizo* ("to sprinkle") is used three times. If by " divers washings" the inspired writer included sprinklings, why did he use a different word when, as everybody knows, he intended to convey the idea of sprinkling? Is there a man under the sun who can tell?

10. *Immersion, it is affirmed, is indecent and dangerous.*

What says Dr. Richard Watson, in his *Theological Institutes*, a work so highly approved by his Methodist brethren? Here is his language: "With all the arrangements of modern times, baptism by immersion is not a decent practice: there is not a female, perhaps, who submits to it who has not a great previous struggle with her delicacy." Again: "Even if immersion had been the original mode of baptizing, we should in the absence of any command on the subject, direct or implied, have thought the church at liberty to accommodate the manner of applying water to the body in the name of the Trinity, in which the essence of the rite consists, to different climates and manners; but it is satisfactory to discover that all the attempts made to impose upon Christians a practice repulsive to the feelings, dangerous to the health, and offensive to delicacy is destitute of all scriptural authority and of really primitive practice." *

Immersion "not a decent practice"! Yet the Methodist "Discipline" authorizes it! Does it authorize an indecent practice? It recognizes immersion as valid baptism, and its validity must arise from the appointment of Jesus Christ. It cannot be valid unless he has appointed it. Will Methodists dare say that one of Christ's appointments "is not a decent practice"? Will they say that this "practice" is

* Vol. ii., pp. 648, 660, New York edition.

DISTINCTIVE PRINCIPLES OF BAPTISTS. 157

"repulsive to the feelings" and "offensive to delicacy"? Can it be "repulsive to the feelings" of Christ's friends to do what he has commanded? No "female," it seems, "submits to" immersion without "a great previous struggle with her delicacy"! Ah, indeed! Baptists who practise immersion know nothing of this "great struggle." The temptation to write something severe on this point is quite strong; but I resist it, and only say that persons who see "indecency" or "indelicacy" in immersion are vulgar-minded. The "indecency" and the "indelicacy" are in them, not in the ordinance of Christ.

In the foregoing extract from Watson, where he refers to "the church" as "at liberty to accommodate the manner of applying water to the body in the name of the Trinity," the discerning reader will detect the *germ* of Popery. Ah, that "liberty to accommodate"! How mischievous has been its operation! It led Calvin to say that, though immersion was the primitive practice, "the church did grant liberty to herself, since the beginning, to change the rites somewhat, excepting the substance." It led Watson to say that "if immersion had been the original mode of baptizing" the church would be "at liberty to accommodate the manner of applying" the water. In the last decade it led Dean Stanley to refer to the substitution of sprinkling in the place of immersion (admitted by him to have been the ancient baptism) as "the triumph of common sense and convenience over the bondage of form and custom." Alas! the exercise of this assumed "liberty to accommodate"—that is, to deviate from the order appointed by Christ—resulted in the establishment of the Romish hierarchy, and has led to the formation of every Pedobaptist church under heaven. This fact is intensely suggestive.

I have now examined the most prominent objections of Pedobaptists to immersion. Whatever else may be said of these objections, it cannot be said that they have *weight*. They are light as the thin air—lighter than vanity. They indicate the weakness of the cause they are intended to support. An examination of them must confirm Baptists in the belief of their distinctive principle which has now been considered—namely, that THE IMMERSION IN WATER OF A BELIEVER IN CHRIST IS ESSENTIAL TO BAPTISM—SO ESSENTIAL THAT WITHOUT IT THERE IS NO BAPTISM.

CHAPTER III.

BAPTISTS HOLD THAT, ACCORDING TO THE SCRIPTURAL ORDER, PERSONS MUST COME FIRST TO CHRIST AND THEN TO THE CHURCH AND ITS ORDINANCES.

IN the foregoing pages we have seen who are subjects of baptism and what is the baptismal act. The act must not be performed until there are subjects to receive it, and the subjects must first have come to Christ. This Baptist principle is not always made so distinctly prominent as the two principles already discussed; and probably the reason is that it is supposed to be involved in them. It is, however, entitled to separate consideration, though this chapter need not be so long as either of the preceding ones.

Baptists are distinguished from all other religious denominations by their belief that no one is eligible to a church relation who has not first been brought into a personal, spiritual relation to Christ by faith in his name. In this belief we see such a divergence of views between Baptists and others as makes compromise and harmony impossible. The question is broad and deep, embracing the New-Testament doctrine of a spiritual church. If Pedobaptists are right in their conception of a church, Baptists are wrong; if Baptists are right, Pedobaptists are wrong. The antagonism between them is not incidental or accidental, but essential and inevitable. It may be said—it need not be said in any offensive sense—that the antagonism involves a war of extermination. That is to say, if the Pedobaptist view of a church and its ordinances should be so carried into effect as to attain universal prevalence, the Baptist view would be banished from the earth; if the Baptist view of a church and its ordinances should universally prevail, the Pedobaptist view must become obsolete. The two views are destructive of each other. But it is time to notice the scriptural order announced at the head of this chapter.

SECTION I.

The doctrine of baptismal regeneration reverses this order.

Incredible as it may appear, there are multitudes who believe in baptismal regeneration. Possibly, Roman Catholics would prefer saying that they believe in baptismal salvation. They regard baptism as essential to the salvation of infants. They are baptized that they may be introduced into the church, out of which it is believed that there is no salvation. The doctrine of Romanists is that "infants receive in baptism spiritual grace;" which, of course, means that they are made the subjects of grace and salvation. This reception of "spiritual grace" is independent of personal faith in Christ, for unconscious infants cannot exercise faith. This is virtually admitted in the provision of sponsors in the administration of baptism to infants. Godfathers and godmothers, by a sort of pious fiction, personate the infants and promise for them; or rather the infants themselves are represented, in utter disregard of truth and of fact, as promising to renounce the devil and all his works. All this is an inversion of the scriptural order, which requires a personal coming to Christ, and *through him* to the church and its ordinances. The Romish plan is for persons, whether infants or adults, to be brought, by means of baptismal salvation, into the church, and thus to Christ.

The Lutheran view of baptism does not differ materially from the Romish dogma. In the Augsburg Confession, drawn up by Melanchthon in 1530, and recognized as the "Creed of the German Reformers," the "grace of God" is said to be "offered through baptism." The Baptists—styled "Anabaptists"—are condemned because they affirm that "children are saved without baptism." The doctrine that baptism is "necessary and effectual to salvation"—Dr. Hodge being judge—has been "softened down" by Lutheran theologians; so that they now say that "baptism is ordinarily necessary." Dr. Krauth, in his learned volume *The Conservative Reformation and its Theology* (p. 431), expresses himself thus: "On God's part it [baptism] is not so necessary that he may not, in an extraordinary case, reach, in an extraordinary way, what baptism is his ordinary way of accomplishing. Food is ordinarily necessary to human life; so that the father who voluntarily withholds food from his child is at heart its murderer. Yet food is not so absolutely necessary to human life that God may not sustain life without it."

The "softening down," according to this extract, is not very great. The position assumed is that salvation without baptism is " an extraordinary case "—so much so as to be miraculous, for the illustration given teaches that God may sustain human life without food; which, of course, would be nothing less than a miracle. It cannot be denied, then, that Lutherans believe that baptism is ordinarily necessary to salvation, and that salvation without it is exceptional and abnormal. It follows, according to this view, that infants are introduced into the " church " and put into a saved state without first coming to Christ.

The Protestant Episcopal Church holds the doctrine of baptismal regeneration. This is evident, from what the minister, after baptizing an infant, is required to say—namely, " We yield thee hearty thanks, most

DISTINCTIVE PRINCIPLES OF BAPTISTS. 163

merciful Father, that it hath pleased thee to regenerate *this infant* with thy Holy Spirit, to receive *him* for thine own *child* by adoption, and to incorporate *him* into thy holy church."

It will be observed that it is taken for granted that regeneration has taken place, and that it has been effected by the Holy Spirit: "It hath pleased thee to regenerate." The same doctrine of baptismal regeneration is recognized in the Catechism, in which the child (before " confirmation ") gives his or her name. Then the question is asked, "Who gave you this name?" The answer is, "My sponsors in baptism; wherein I was made a member of Christ, the child of God, and an inheritor of the kingdom of heaven." It would be difficult to conceive how baptism can do more than is here attributed to it. All the possibilities of present and eternal salvation are involved in the expressions "a member of Christ," "the child of God," and "an inheritor of the kingdom of heaven."

That it may be seen that I do no injustice to the teachings of the "Book of Common Prayer" I quote from a prominent Episcopal minister, Dr. Richard Newton, rector of the church of the Epiphany in Philadelphia. In a letter published in the *Life of Bishop Cummins* (p. 354) Dr. Newton says: "And after all that can be said of the different theories that may be forced on the words 'regenerate,' etc., in our service for infant baptism, the natural, legitimate construction to put upon it—the construction which any honest jury of twelve men with no theory to maintain on the subject would put upon it—is that it *does* teach the horrible dogma that spiritual regeneration is inseparably connected with the use of baptism."

This testimony is very strong, but its truth is equal to its strength. It furnishes cause for deep regret that millions among Romanists, Lutherans, and Episcopalians ascribe to baptism a saving efficacy, and hold what Dr. Newton terms a "horrible dogma." This "dogma" is at war with the distinctive principle of Baptists that persons must come first to Christ, and then to the church and its ordinances. The scriptural order is reversed by all the advocates of baptismal regeneration.

SECTION II.

The practice of infant baptism reverses this order.

The evils of infant baptism are not confined to the theory of baptismal regeneration. They develop themselves most appallingly in connection with this theory; but they are to be seen wherever and for whatever purpose infant baptism is practised. It is itself a great evil, and great evils result from it. The following language of the late godly Dr. J. Newton Brown, though strong, is not too strong: "Infant baptism is an error from beginning to end; corrupt in theory and corrupting in practice; born in superstition, cradled in fear, nursed in ignorance, supported by fraud, and spread by force; doomed to die in the light of historical investigation, and its very memory to be loathed in all future ages by a disabused church. In the realms of despotism it has shed the blood of martyrs in torrents; that blood cries against it to heaven, and a long-suffering God will yet be the terrible avenger."*

In a note Dr. Brown says: "In no boastful spirit, but in the spirit of a martyr before God—stung by the solemn conviction of duty after thirty-five years of earnest and impartial investigation on this subject to speak out 'the truth, the whole truth, and nothing but the truth'—we nail these THESES to the door of every Pedobaptist church in Christendom and challenge all the Christian scholarship of the age not to ignore, evade, or deny them, but to face the inevitable trial, summon the witnesses, sift the evidence, and, if it can, disprove all or any one of them. And may God help the right!"

While Presbyterians and Methodists generally disavow all sympathy with the doctrine of baptismal regeneration, they are decided in their espousal and advocacy of infant baptism. It is strange that the spirituality of the Christian Dispensation does not lead them to give up the practice. It is pre-eminently a

* Essay prefixed to *Memorials of Baptist Martyrs*, p. 13.

spiritual economy. How Jesus exalts spiritual relations above those which are natural, we clearly see in Mark iii. 35: "For whosoever shall do the will of God, the same is my brother, and my sister, and mother." Paul said, "We know no man after the flesh;" but infant baptism is a recognition of the relations of the flesh. Infants, it is claimed, are proper subjects of baptism because they are descended from believing parents. This view is earnestly defended by Presbyterians, who insist that at least one of the parents of the infant to be baptized must be a believer. But the relation between parents and baptized infants is *natural*, whereas all the relations which the gospel recognizes are spiritual. Parents must first believe in Christ, in order to be brought into a spiritual relation with him; but their faith does not create a spiritual relation to their children. There can be no such relation until the children believe. All believers are spiritually related to one another, and the reason is that they are all in spiritual union with Christ. The relation to him is supreme, and out of it spring all subordinate spiritual relations. But Pedobaptists, in the practice of infant baptism, proceed on the supposition that the existence of a *natural* relation between them and their children entitles the latter to a Christian ordinance. The supposition is entirely gratuitous, and in positive conflict with the spirituality of the Christian economy. There is between parents and children no relation, whether natural or spiritual, that gives children the right to church-membership. This is plain as to the natural relation. It is equally so as to the spiritual relation, in view of the fact that it is union with Christ by faith which is a prerequisite to baptism and church-membership. Hence, *believing* children possess this prerequisite though their parents are dead. It is their relation to Christ that decides the matter. The reference here is, of course, to children who have reached accountable years. As to unconscious infants, it is one of the strangest of strange things that they can be thought eligible to baptism and church-membership. This view is held, and can be held, by those only who reverse one of the distinctive principles of Baptists, claimed by them to be a distinctive principle of the New Testament—namely, *That persons must come first to Christ, and then to the church and its ordinances.* Christ's positive and gracious command is, "Come unto me." He says, "He that cometh to me shall never hunger; and he that believeth on me shall never thirst." He complains of the Jews: "And ye will not come to me, that ye might have life." It is manifest from these forms of expression that "coming to Christ" is a matter of supreme importance. It has an essential connection with the salvation of the soul. Coming to Christ is believing on him, and faith creates spiritual union with him: "Being justified by faith, we have peace with God through our Lord Jesus Christ." The gospel permits nothing to come between Christ and sinners. Their first business is to receive him. They do this by an act of personal faith. He is a personal Saviour, and the act of faith is a personal act. There is no act more intensely personal—not even the act of dying. There is no such thing as believing in Christ by proxy, but every one must believe for himself, even as every one must die for himself. Now, it is those only who have come to Christ by believing on him that have anything to do with the church and its ordinances. A New-Testament church is a spiritual brotherhood the members of which are the subjects of spiritual life, and the ordinances of the gospel are designed for spiritual persons. The opposite view is fraught with evil, for it changes the order which Christ has established. It permits persons to come to the church and its ordinances before they come to Christ. Baptists regard this as disastrous heresy, and utter their earnest protest against it. They have stood alone in the centuries past, and they stand alone now, in advocacy of the great principle, CHRIST FIRST, THEN THE CHURCH AND ITS ORDINANCES.

CHAPTER IV.

BAPTISTS BELIEVE THAT A SCRIPTURAL CHURCH IS A LOCAL CONGREGATION OF BAPTIZED BELIEVERS INDEPENDENT, UNDER CHRIST, OF THE STATE AND OF EVERY OTHER CHURCH, HAVING IN ITSELF AUTHORITY TO DO WHATEVER A CHURCH CAN OF RIGHT DO.

IT requires but little reflection to see that the principle here announced is peculiar to Baptists. No other religious denomination holds it—certainly not in its entirety. The important question, however, is whether the New Testament sustains this principle; for if it does not, the principle possesses no value. It will be observed that my reference is to the New Testament, for it would be absurd to go to the Old Testament to ascertain the nature of a Christian Church. In the matter of church-building, as well as in other things, Jesus said to the apostles, "Teaching them [the disciples] to observe all things whatsoever I have commanded you."

SECTION I.

A scriptural church a local congregation of baptized believers.

The Greek term *ekklesia*—translated "church" more than a hundred times in the New Testament (rendered "assembly" three times)—is compounded of two words literally meaning "to call out of." I shall not attempt to show how this meaning received a practical illustration when assemblies were called out among the Greeks. My present purpose is answered by the statement that in apostolic times a church was composed of persons who had been called out from the world, even as Christ chose his apostles "out of the world." They had been called from the bondage of sin into the liberty of the gospel; from spiritual darkness into the light of salvation; from the dominion of unbelief into the realm of faith; from an heirship of wrath to an heirship of glory. This was true of the members of the first churches. Brought by the Holy Spirit into a new relation to God through Christ, they were prepared for church-relations and church-membership. This preparation was moral, consisting of "repentance toward God and faith toward our Lord Jesus Christ." But repentance and faith are exercises of the mind, and are consequently invisible. They are private transactions between God and the soul. The world knows not of them. Churches, however, are visible organizations. This being the case, there must be some visible ceremonial qualification for membership. This qualification is baptism. There can, according to the Scriptures, be no visible church without baptism. An observance of this ordinance is the believer's first public act of obedience to Christ. Regeneration, repentance, and faith are private matters that take place in the unseen depths of the heart. They involve internal piety, but of this piety there must be an external manifestation. This manifestation is made in baptism. This is "the good profession" made by a most significant symbolic act. The penitent, regenerate believer is baptized "into the name of the Father, and of the Son, and of the Holy Spirit." There is a visible, symbolic expression of a new relation to the three Persons of the Godhead—a relation really entered into in repentance, faith, and regeneration.

That baptized believers are the only persons eligible to church-membership is clear from the whole tenor of the Acts of the Apostles and of the Apostolic Epistles. Everywhere it is seen that baptism preceded church-relations; nor is there an intimation that it was possible for an unbaptized person to be a church-member. On this point, however, there is no controversy between Baptists and Pedobaptists, for both believe in the priority of baptism to church-membership. The difference between them is on the question, What is baptism? The Baptist answer to this question has been given in the preceding part of this volume. According to that answer, *baptism is the immersion in water of a believer in Jesus Christ.* If, then, a church is a congregation of baptized believers, it is a congregation of immersed believers. An unimmersed congregation, therefore, even if a congregation of believers, is not a New-Testament church. Baptists do not deny that there are pious men and women in Pedobaptist churches, so called, but they do deny that these churches are formed according to the New-Testament model. They are without baptism, and, to use the words of a very distinguished Pedobaptist, Dr. E. D. Griffin, "where there is no baptism, there are no visible churches."* Even if Pedobaptists practised immersion, and immersion only, the introduction of the infant element into their churches would vitiate their claim to recognition as New-Testament churches. The infant element must predominate over the adult element, in obedience to the law of increase in population; which law renders children more numerous than parents. Surely, as Pedobaptists practise an uncom-

---

* His celebrated *Letter on Communion*, reviewed by Dr. Ripley, may be seen in the Boston edition of J. G. Fuller *On Communion* also in the *American Baptist Magazine* for September, 1829.

manded ceremony instead of baptism—on unscriptural subjects instead of on believers—their churches can lay no claim to conformity to the New-Testament standard of church organization. They are not congregations of baptized believers. There can be no ecclesiastic fellowship between them and Baptists, for the latter hold most tenaciously that a scriptural church is a local congregation of baptized believers. That a church is a *local* congregation needs no elaborate proof. The fact is sufficiently indicated by the use of the word in both its singular and its plural form. We read of "the church at Jerusalem," "the church of God which is at Corinth," "the church of the Thessalonians," "the church of Ephesus," "the church in Smyrna," etc. Nor is it to be supposed that it required a large number of persons to constitute a church. Paul refers to Aquila and Priscilla and "the church that is in their house," to Nymphas and "the church which is in his house;" while in his letter to Philemon he says, "to the church in thy house." A congregation of saints organized according to the New Testament, whether that congregation is large or small, is a church.

The inspired writers, too, use the term "churches" in the plural; and, as if for ever to preclude the idea of a church commensurate with a province, a kingdom, or an empire, they say "the churches of Galatia," "the churches of Macedonia," "the churches of Asia," "the churches of Judea." In reference to an organization in a city or town or house, the singular "church" is used; but when regions of country are mentioned, we have "churches," in the plural. Wherever Christianity prevailed in apostolic times, there was a plurality of churches.

SECTION II.

The Lord's Supper observed by local churches.

The churches composed, as they are, of Christ's baptized disciples meet for the worship of their Lord. "Not forsaking the assembling of ourselves together" is the language addressed to Christians in apostolic times. Among the duties and the privileges of a congregation of baptized believers in Christ is included a commemoration of his death at his Table. Every local church is required to observe this ordinance. Its obligation to do so is inseparable from its independence; and the doctrine of church independence will be developed in future sections of this chapter. The ordinances of the gospel are placed by Christ in the custody of his churches. They dare not change them in any respect; to change them would be disloyalty to their Lord. They have no legislative power; they are simply executive democracies required to carry into effect the will of their Head. Who but his churches can be expected to preserve the integrity and the purity of the ordinances of the Lord Jesus? These ordinances are to be kept as they were delivered to the churches and received by them. This is indispensable to the maintenance of gospel order.

What Paul writes to the Corinthians (1 Cor. xi. 20-34) clearly indicates the necessity of coming together "to eat the Lord's Supper." True, he refers to certain irregularities, which he severally condemns; but when he asks, "Despise ye the church of God?" he refers to its members, not in their individual, but in their collective, capacity—the congregation of God. So, in verses 33, 34, the words "when ye come together to eat, tarry one for another," and "that ye come not together unto condemnation," show beyond doubt that the assembling of the church was requisite to the celebration of the Lord's Supper. It is a church ordinance, and therefore Baptists oppose any and every attempt to administer it privately to individuals without church sanction.

What was true of the Corinthian church as to the "coming together" of its members to commemorate the death of Christ was doubtless true of all other churches of that period. It would be absurd to suppose that there was a capricious diversity in the customs of the churches. We may therefore assume that there was uniformity.

With regard to the Lord's Supper there are different

views held by different religious denominations. Roman Catholics believe in what they call Transubstantiation—that is, that by the consecration of the priest the bread and the wine are changed into the real body and the real blood of Christ. This doctrine defies all reasonable credence, and can be accepted only by a voracious credulity. It requires a renunciation of common sense to believe that when Jesus took bread into his hands, that bread became his body; so that he held his body in his hands! The statement of such a dogma is its sufficient exposure.

Lutherans, while they dissent from the Romish view, advocate what they call Consubstantiation. By this they mean that in the Lord's Supper the body and the blood of Christ are really present in the bread and the wine. While this view differs from the Romish, it is equally mysterious and scarcely less incredible; for it demands the impossible belief that the body of Christ is not only present in many places on earth at the same time, but that it is also in heaven. Surely the body of Christ is not omnipresent.

Episcopalians and Methodists, as well as Romanists and Lutherans, receive kneeling the bread and the wine in the Lord's Supper. The posture is an unnatural one, and the custom of kneeling no doubt has an historical connection with Transubstantiation—that is to say, when the dogma was accepted as true, the bread and the wine were considered suitable objects of adoration. Hence the kneeling attitude was assumed by Romanists, transmitted by them to Episcopalians, and from them inherited by Methodists. It is strange, in view of the idolatrous origin of the custom of kneeling, that it is continued by those who abjure idolatry. This by the way.

There is one thing in the service of Episcopalians and Methodists which must ever impress Baptists as very strange: The minister, in delivering the bread to each person, says, "The body of our Lord Jesus Christ, which was given for thee, preserve thy body and soul unto everlasting life." In giving the cup he says, "The blood of our Lord Jesus Christ, which was shed for thee, preserve thy body and soul unto everlasting life." * This may not be, but it seems to be, a prayer offered to the body and the blood of Christ, which are invoked to preserve unto everlasting life the body and the soul of the person addressed. Prayer to Christ is eminently proper, for it is justified by the example of the dying Stephen; but prayer to the body and the blood of Christ is utterly indefensible.

Presbyterians are nearer right in their views of the Lord's Supper than are the denominations to which I

---

* The Methodist "Discipline" transposes the terms "body" and "soul."

have referred. They do not kneel and they make prominent the commemorative feature of the ordinance. True, they call it a "sealing ordinance;" and these words Baptists vainly try to understand. What is sealed? "The covenant of grace," they say. How is this? They say also that "baptism seals" it. Has it two seals? Among men covenants are invalid without seals. Is the covenant of grace invalid for purposes of salvation unless the seals of baptism and the Lord's Supper are appended to it? Presbyterians will hardly answer in the affirmative. The truth is the New Testament never refers to baptism and the Lord's Supper as "sealing ordinances," and for the best reason: It teaches that believers are "sealed by the Holy Spirit unto the day of redemption." If the Holy Spirit seals, there is security; and there is something wrong in the theology which makes baptism and the Lord's Supper "sealing ordinances."

Baptists hold that, as the Lord's Supper is a church-ordinance, the supreme prerequisite to it is church-membership. Baptism, it is true, is often referred to as a prerequisite, and so it is, but only in the sense that it is a prerequisite to church-membership. The members of every local church can claim it as a right to come to the Lord's Table in that church, but in no other. They may, through fraternal courtesy, be admitted to the Lord's Supper in sister-churches, but to demand admittance *as a right* would be an assault on church independence. This is a matter so plain that it is needless to dwell on it. It sometimes creates a smile when it is said that Baptists are more liberal in their views and practice in regard to the Lord's Supper than are any other people; but it is true. It is true in the sense that they believe that all whom they baptize and receive into church-membership are entitled to seats at the Lord's Table; and it is true in the sense that they welcome to that Table all whom they baptize. They dare not sever from each other the two ordinances of the gospel. Of what other denomination can this be said? I refer to the denominations of Protestant Christendom. Among Episcopalians, Lutherans, Presbyterians, and Methodists baptism and the Lord's Supper are put asunder— that is to say, this is true of "baptized children" as distinguished from "communicants." With Episcopalians and Lutherans these "baptized children," so called, are kept from the Lord's Table until they receive the rite of "Confirmation." It is not possible to give a good reason for this practice; for if through "sponsors" they are entitled to baptism, they are also entitled to the Lord's Supper. Presbyterians require in the "baptized children" evidence of personal piety before they are allowed to come to the Lord's Table, and Methodists, to say the least, insist that there shall be "a desire to flee from the wrath to come." The argument against inviting infants is that infants cannot "discern the body and blood of the Lord Jesus." This is doubtless true; but it is equally true that they cannot discern the spiritual significance of baptism. If the inability to "discern" is a bar to the Lord's Table, it should also be a bar to the Lord's baptism. There can be no good reason for severing the ordinances of the gospel. Those who are entitled to baptism are entitled to the Lord's Supper. There is an interference with scriptural order whenever the two ordinances are disjoined. The interference cannot be justified. Baptists, therefore, say that the Lord's Supper is not scripturally observed among Pedobaptists. They have neither scriptural baptism nor scriptural church-membership, and there cannot be a scriptural administration of the Lord's Supper. In addition to this, they withhold from a large number—perhaps a majority—of those who, in their judgment, are baptized the Lord's Supper. This is a great inconsistency. It must be said, however, that if the ordinances were not sundered—that is, if all baptized by Pedobaptists were permitted to come to the Lord's Supper—the service would be vitiated by the presence of a majority composed of unbelievers and of those incapable of believing. In view of such considerations as these, it will readily be seen why Baptists believe that Pedobaptists fail to observe the Lord's

DISTINCTIVE PRINCIPLES OF BAPTISTS. 181

Supper according to the New Testament, even as they fail to administer New-Testament baptism.

On the other hand, it is a distinctive Baptist principle that a scriptural church is a congregation of baptized believers in Christ, whose duty and privilege it is "to eat the Lord's Supper." All the members of such a church are required to commemorate their Lord's death. They are united to him by faith in his name, and through him, by spiritual ties, to one another, while their baptism has incorporated them into one body, and their partaking of "one bread" (1 Cor. x. 17) is a symbol of their unity.

Baptists detach from the Lord's Supper every idea of Transubstantiation, Consubstantiation, ritual efficacy, sealing virtue, etc., and consider it a memorial of Christ's death. Its commemorative office is that which constitutes its supreme distinction. Everything else connected with it is secondary and incidental. "This do in remembrance of me," said Jesus in instituting the ordinance on the night of the betrayal. In the eating of the broken bread he requires that his crucified body be remembered; in the drinking of the cup he enjoins a remembrance of his blood. That the faculty of memory is specially exercised concerning the death of Christ in the sacred Supper is manifest from 1 Cor. xi. 26: "For as often as ye eat this bread, and drink this cup, ye do shew the Lord's death till he come." We do not show his birth or baptism or burial or resurrection or ascension, but his death. If ever the tragedy of Calvary should engross the thoughts of the Christian to the exclusion of every other subject, it is when he sits at the Table of the Lord. Then memory must reproduce the scenes of the crucifixion and so hold them up to the mind that Christ is "evidently set forth crucified." Then in the eating of the bread and the drinking of the cup the body and the blood of the Lord are "spiritually discerned," and the ordinance, by the presence of the Holy Spirit, becomes a rich blessing to the soul. It becomes the means of strengthening faith in Christ and of increasing love to him; while memory goes back to his death, and hope looks to his second coming, when his personal presence will supersede the necessity of any symbol to promote a remembrance of him.

SECTION III.

Definition of church independence.

There are three prominent forms of church-government, indicated by the terms Episcopacy, Presbyterianism, and Independency.

Episcopacy recognizes the right of bishops to preside over districts of country, and one of its fundamental doctrines is that a bishop is officially superior to an elder. Of course, in that church, a modern bishop has under his charge the "inferior clergy" as well as "the laity;" for it is insisted that the "ordaining power" and the "right to rule" belong to the episcopal office. In apostolic times "bishop" and "pastor" were terms of equivalent import. The elders of the church of Ephesus are styled (Acts xx. 28) "overseers"—in the original, *episcopoi*, the word generally translated "bishop," if, indeed, "bishop" may be called a translation. It is so evident from the Scriptures that bishops and elders are identical that it is the greatest folly to call it in question. This, however, is not the place to enlarge on the topic.

Presbyterianism recognizes two classes of elders—*preaching* elders and *ruling* elders. The pastor and the ruling elders of a congregation constitute what is called the "Session of the church." The "Session" transacts the business of the church, receives, dismisses, and excludes members. From the decision of a Session there is an appeal to Presbytery, which is composed of preaching and ruling elders. From the action of a Presbytery there lies an appeal to Synod, and from the adjudications of Synod there is an appeal to the General Assembly, whose decrees are final and irresistible. These Presbyteries, Synods, and General Assemblies are often termed "church courts," "judicatories of the church."

The friends of Presbyterianism, no doubt, deem their

form of government most expedient and satisfactory; but to prove it scriptural must be as difficult as to show that baptism has been substituted for circumcision. Where is it intimated in the Scriptures that there is an appeal from the lower to the higher "church courts"? While Presbyterians, therefore, talk and write about the *expediency* of their form of government, they ought to say nothing of its *scripturalness*. It is unquestionably a better government than the Episcopal, but it is not the government established by Jesus Christ. It is easily seen that Episcopacy and Presbyterianism imply that many local congregations enter representatively into the composition of what is called "the church." We, therefore, often hear of the "Episcopal Church of the United States of America," the "Presbyterian Church of the United States." The local religious communities in all parts of the nation where Episcopacy prevails are considered as constituting the "Episcopal Church." So of Presbyterianism and Methodism. *The Baptist Church of the United States* is a form of expression which ought never to be used—which can never be used with propriety. There are more than twenty thousand Baptist *churches* in the United States, but they do not constitute one great Baptist Church of the United States. They differ materially and fundamentally from Episcopal, Presbyterian, and Methodist churches. They are all independent of the state.

This, however, is true of all religious denominations in this country; for the genius of our republic does not tolerate "Union between Church and State." But it deserves special notice that Baptists, with their views of the *spirituality* of New-Testament churches, could not, under any form of government, enter into an alliance with the state. Episcopacy is established by law in England, Presbyterianism in Scotland, Lutheranism in Germany and Sweden and Denmark. When Jesus stood before Pilate, he said, "My kingdom is not of this world." The view which Baptists have of these words is entirely hostile to the doctrine of a state-church. Their appreciation of "soul-liberty" is so great that they can allow no interference with it. They are the friends of civil government, and believe any form of government better than anarchy. They pray for civil rulers, whether they be presidents or kings, but deny the right of the civil power to intrude into the spiritual realm of conscience. Their blood, often shed by their persecutors, has often testified to the sincerity of their belief. Their views find expression in the stanza:

> "Let Cæsar's dues be ever paid
> To Cæsar and his throne;
> But consciences and souls were made
> For God, the Lord, alone."

Churches formed according to the New-Testament

model are not only independent of the state, but in matters pertaining to government they are independent of one another. They are interdependent only in the sense involved in mutual fellowship; and their mutual influence is not to be lightly esteemed, for it answers valuable purposes. But it must not be forgotten that every local congregation of baptized believers united in church worship and work is as complete a church as ever existed, and is perfectly competent to do whatever a church can of right do. It is as complete as if it were the only church in the world.

It follows from the doctrine of church independence that no church is at liberty to interfere with the internal affairs of another. Every Baptist church is an independent and a pure democracy. The idea of independence should be earnestly cherished, while that of consolidation should be as earnestly deprecated. Agreeably to the view now presented, we read in the New Testament of "the *churches* of Judea," "the *churches* of Galatia," "the *churches* of Macedonia," but we never read of the *church* of Judea and of other provinces. There is not the remotest reference to a *church* commensurate with a province, with a kingdom, or with an empire. This view of church extension and consolidation was *post*-apostolic—manifestly so.

There are no people who recognize more fully than do Baptists the fact that the phrase "kingdom of

Christ" implies that he is King, Monarch, Autocrat. In ordaining the laws of his kingdom he did not allow the impertinent interference of men. There is no human legislation in the kingdom of Christ. Churches organized according to the New Testament are required to execute the laws of Christ. To do this they must first decide what those laws are. It may be said, therefore, that the churches of Christ are invested with *judicial* and *executive* power, but they have no *legislative* power. Ecclesiastical legislation—such as is permitted in many Pedobaptist organizations—is abhorrent to the spirit of the gospel. Churches are executive democracies organized to carry out the sovereign will of their Lord and King.

The Baptist view of this matter is forcibly expressed in the language of the late J. M. Peck, D. D. Referring to Baptists, he says:

"Their theory of church government embraces two great and apparently opposite principles.

"*First.* That the *kingdom of Christ*, in its visible form on earth, *is a pure monarchy*. Christ is King and Lawgiver. He needs not the aid of man, nor will he endure human legislation in any form. He has not merely given a few vague and general rules, and left his people to work out all the discordant plans of government that prevail at this moment in Christendom. Both by precept and in the inspired records of the primitive churches there are examples for every class of cases that necessity ever requires. The *legislation* in his kingdom is all divine.

"*Secondly.* His kingdom, in its organized state of small communities, each managing its own affairs in its own vicinage, is a *pure democracy.* THE PEOPLE —THE WHOLE PEOPLE—in each community choose their own officers, receive and expel members, conduct all business as a body politic, decide on all questions of discipline, and observe all the institutions of Christ. Were they to institute a *representative* or any other form of government, they would depart from the law-book and soon be involved in as many difficulties as their neighbors."*

In accordance with these principles, the governmental power of churches is, under Christ, with the members, including pastors and deacons. These officers, however, can do nothing without the concurrence of the membership. It results of necessity from church independence that a majority must rule, that the power of a church cannot be transferred or alienated, and that church action is final. The power of a church cannot be delegated. There may be messengers of a church, but not delegates. No church can empower any man or any body of men to do anything which will impair its independency.

* *Christian Repository* (1853), vol. ii., pp. 47, 48.

These are highly-important principles; and, while the existence of the independent form of church government depends on their recognition and application, it is an inquiry of vital moment, Does the New Testament recognize these principles? For if it does not, whatever may be said in commendation of them they possess no binding force. I refer to the New Testament, because it would be unjustifiable to go to the Old to ascertain the form of government established for *Christian* churches. Jesus Christ, in instructing the apostles how to train the baptized disciples, says, " Teaching them to observe all things whatsoever I have commanded you " (Matt. xxviii. 20). He does not say " all things that Moses commanded," but " all things whatsoever I have commanded." The apostles enjoyed his teaching during his ministry, and the " forty days " between his resurrection and his ascension he employed in speaking to them of " the things pertaining to the kingdom of God " (Acts i. 3). It may be said that Paul was not with Christ during his ministry, and that he did not enjoy the advantage of the " forty days' " instruction. This is true; but his deficiencies, as compared with those of the other apostles, were evidently supplied by direct revelations from heaven. It will be seen, therefore, that the apostles themselves had no *discretionary* power. They were to teach the observance of all things their Lord and Master had "commanded"—no more, no less. Whatever they taught under the influence of inspiration must have accorded with the teachings of Christ. Whatever they did as inspired men may be considered as done by him.

SECTION IV.

The churches of the New Testament received, excluded, and restored members.

In proof and in illustration of this proposition the following facts are submitted.

In Rom. xiv. 1 it is written: "Him that is weak in the faith receive ye, but not to doubtful disputations." What is the meaning of the first clause of this verse? Its import is obviously this: Receive into your fellowship, and treat as a Christian, the man who is weak in faith. The paraphrase of Mr. Barnes is, "Admit to your society or fellowship, receive him kindly." There is unquestionably a command: "RECEIVE YE." To whom is this command addressed? To bishops? It is not. To the "Session of the church," composed of the pastor and the "ruling elders"? No. To whom, then? To the very persons to whom the Epistle was addressed; and it was written "to all that be in Rome, beloved of God, called to be saints" (i. 7). No ingenuity can torture this language into a command given to the officers of the church in Rome. The members of the church—whose designation was "saints"—were addressed, and they were commanded to "receive the weak in faith." It was their business to decide who should be admitted into their brotherhood; and Paul, under the impulses of inspiration, says, "Him that is weak in the faith receive ye." It was, of course, their duty to withhold their fellowship from those who had no faith. The right of the apostolic churches to withdraw their fellowship from unworthy members (2 Thess. iii. 6) plainly implies their right to receive persons of proper qualifications into their fellowship. It is inconceivable that they had the authority to exclude, but not to receive, members.

I now proceed to show that the New-Testament churches exercised the right of excluding unworthy members. In 1 Cor. v. 1-5 we read as follows: "It is reported commonly that there is fornication among you, and such fornication as is not so much as named among the Gentiles, that one should have his father's wife. And ye are puffed up, and have not rather mourned, that he that hath done this deed might be taken away from among you. For I verily, as absent in body, but present in spirit, have judged already, as though I were present, concerning him that hath so done this deed, in the name of our Lord Jesus Christ, when ye are gathered together, and my spirit, with the power of our Lord Jesus Christ, to deliver such a one unto Satan for the destruction of the flesh, that the spirit may be saved in the day of the Lord Jesus."

It is quite worthy of remark that, while Paul "judged" that the incestuous member ought to be excluded from the church, *he* did not exclude him. He had no right to do so, and did not claim the right.

The same apostle said to the "churches of Galatia," "I would they were even cut off which trouble you" (Gal. v. 12); but he did not cut them off, though he desired it to be done and advised that it should be done.

It is worthy of notice too that the members of the Corinthian church could not, in their *individual capacity*, exclude the incestuous man. It was necessary to their action in the premises that they should be "gathered together." They must assemble as a church and exemplify the doctrine of a pure democracy. Thus assembling, "the power of our Lord Jesus Christ" was to be with them. They were to act by his authority and to execute his will; for he makes it incumbent on his churches to administer discipline. In the last verse of the chapter referred to, Paul says: "Put away from among yourselves that wicked person." Here is a command, given by an inspired man, requiring the exclusion of an unworthy member of the church at Corinth. To whom was the command addressed? To the official members of the church?

No, but "unto the church of God which is at Corinth, to them that are sanctified in Christ Jesus, called to be saints."

The right of a church to exclude disorderly persons from its fellowship is recognized in these words: "Now we command you, brethren, in the name of our Lord Jesus Christ, that ye withdraw yourselves from every brother that walketh disorderly" (2 Thess. iii. 6). This command was addressed "to the church of the Thessalonians." To "withdraw" from a "disorderly brother" is the same thing as to exclude him. There is a cessation of church-fellowship.

I have not referred to Matt. xviii. 17, because I shall notice it in another place. The reader will see on examination that the passage clearly shows the power of "the church" to perform the act of excommunication by which the member cut off becomes "as a heathen man and a publican."

It is not more evident that New-Testament churches received and excluded members than that they restored excluded members who gave satisfactory evidence of penitence. In 2 Cor. ii. 6–8 the "incestuous man" is again referred to, as follows: "Sufficient to such a man is this punishment, which was inflicted of many. So that contrariwise ye ought rather to forgive him, and comfort him, lest perhaps such a one should be swallowed up with overmuch sorrow. Wherefore I beseech you that ye would confirm your love toward him."

Paul manages this case with the greatest delicacy and tenderness. He refers to the excluded member without the least allusion to the disgraceful offence for which he was excluded. "Sufficient," says he, "is this punishment"—that is, the object of the exclusion had been accomplished. The church had shown its determination not to connive at sin, and the excluded member had become penitent. But the point under consideration is that the apostle advised the restoration of the penitent offender. Paul could no more restore him to the church than he could exclude him from it; but he says, "I beseech you that ye would confirm your love toward him." The power and the right to restore were with the church, and Paul solicits an exercise of the power and of the right. The great apostle, in saying "I beseech you," bows to the majesty of the doctrine of church independence. He virtually admits that nothing could be done unless the church chose to act.

In this connection one fact should be carefully observed: The power of the Corinthian church to restore this excluded member is unquestionable. The fact which deserves special notice and emphasis is that the power, in apostolic churches, to restore excluded members implies the power of receiving members, and also of expelling the unworthy. Without a first reception there could be no exclusion, and without exclusion there could be no subsequent restoration. Thus the act of restoration irresistibly implies the two previous acts of reception and exclusion. Now, if the New-Testament churches had the power and the right to do these three things, they must have had the power and the right to transact any other business coming before them. Nothing can be of more vital importance to the welfare, and even to the existence, of a church than the reception, the exclusion, and the restoration of members. There are no three acts whose influence on the organic structure and prosperity of a church is so great; and these acts the churches of the New Testament undoubtedly performed.

Here I might let the foundation principle of church independency rest; but there is other proof of the New-Testament recognition of that principle.

SECTION V.
The churches of the New Testament appointed their officers.

In the first chapter of the Acts of the Apostles there is an account of the election of Matthias to the apostleship. He was to succeed Judas the traitor. The most natural inference is that Matthias was chosen by the "one hundred and twenty disciples" mentioned in verse 15. These "disciples" were, no doubt, the church to which the three thousand converts were added on the day of Pentecost. The brethren must have been held in high estimation by Peter if called on, in conjunction with the apostles themselves, to elect a successor to Judas.

In Acts vi. there is reference to the circumstances which originated the office of deacon, and also to the manner in which the first deacons were appointed. We read as follows: "And in those days, when the number of the disciples was multiplied, there arose a murmuring of the Grecians against the Hebrews, because their widows were neglected in the daily ministration. Then the twelve called the multitude of the disciples unto them, and said, It is not reason that we should leave the word of God, and serve tables. Wherefore, brethren, look ye out among you seven men of honest report, full of the Holy Ghost and wisdom, whom we may appoint over this business. But we will give ourselves continually to prayer, and to the ministry of the word. And the saying pleased the whole multitude: and they chose Stephen, a man full of faith and of the Holy Ghost, and Philip, and Prochorus, and Nicanor, and Timon, and Parmenas, and Nicolas, a proselyte of Antioch; whom they set before the apostles: and when they had prayed they laid their hands on them."

It will be seen from this narrative that the apostles referred the matter of grievance to "the multitude of the disciples;" directed the "brethren to look out seven men;" that "the saying pleased the whole multitude;" that "they chose Stephen" and the others. The democracy of the whole arrangement is as clear as the light of day. The people, the whole membership of the church at Jerusalem, were recognized as the responsible source of authority, and they were required to make selection of suitable men. Large as was the number of church-members, they did not, for the sake of convenience, or for any other reason, delegate to a representative few the power to act for them. They knew nothing of a delegation of power. The whole multitude acted.

In Acts xiv. 23 there is mention made of the ordination of elders in every church, as follows: "And when they had ordained them elders in every church, and had prayed with fasting, they commended them to the Lord on whom they believed." Some think that William Tyndale's translation comes nearer to the meaning of the original. With the spelling modernized, it is as follows: "And when they had ordained them seniors by election, in every congregation, after they had prayed and fasted, they commended them to God, on whom they believed." The word in the original here translated "ordained" literally means "to stretch forth the hand," as is the custom in Baptist churches when a vote is taken. Tyndale puts in the words "by election," believing, as he did, that the New-Testament churches elected their elders by the votes of the members. He also states in his *Rights of the Church*—as quoted by Lyman Coleman in his *Apostolical and Primitive Church* (p. 63)—that the Greek word referred to (*cheirotoneo*, from *cheir*, "the hand," and *teino*, "to stretch forth") is interpreted as he interprets it "by Erasmus, Beza, Diodati, and those who translated the Swiss, French, Italian, Belgic, and even English, Bibles, till the Episcopal correction, which leaves out the words, 'by election,' as well as the marginal notes, which affirm that the apostles did not thrust pastors into the church through a lordly superiority, *but chose and placed them there by the voice of the congregation.*"

Every one can imagine why the "Episcopal correction" was made. The words "by election" would give the "laity" an agency and an influence which the "Episcopal clergy" would not willingly allow. The word *cheirotoneo* is used but twice in the New Testament—in the passage under consideration and in 2 Cor. viii. 19. In the latter it is translated "chosen," and the choice was "by the churches." In the former it certainly means that elders were chosen, appointed, not without, but by means of, the suffrages of the churches. Mr. Barnes, in his notes on the passage, well remarks: "It is said, indeed, that Paul and Barnabas did this. But probably all that is meant by it is that they presided in the assembly when the choice was made. It does not mean that they appointed them without consulting the church; but it evidently means that they appointed them in the usual way of appointing officers—by the suffrages of the people."

In view of the facts now presented, it is plain that according to the New Testament the officers of a church are chosen by the church. No one church has the right to choose officers for another. No combination of churches has the right. Every church is as independent in its action as if it were the only church in the world. It will not be forgotten that "elders were ordained in every church." There was, of course, uniformity of custom: all the churches of apostolic times were formed after the same model. That there was diversity in their formation is utterly incredible.

In further support of the principle of Independency, I state the following facts without elaborating them: In the Jerusalem Council of which we are informed in Acts xv., "the whole church," the "brethren," are named in connection with the "apostles and elders:" "Then pleased it the apostles and elders, with the whole church, to send chosen men;" "And they wrote letters by them after this manner: The apostles and elders and brethren send greeting." The members of the church at Jerusalem acted, as well as the apostles and the elders.

The churches of apostolic times sent forth ministers on missionary-tours. When Antioch received the word of God, the church at Jerusalem " sent forth Barnabas, that he should go as far as Antioch" (Acts xi. 22). His labors were successful—" much people was added to the Lord "—and at a subsequent period the church in Antioch sent out Saul and Barnabas, who made a long journey, performed much labor, returned, and reported to the church " all that God had done with them." They "gathered the church together" before they gave an account of their labors.* With what deferential respect did these ministers treat the church that sent them forth! Their example is worthy of imitation by ministers of all generations.

The apostles, so far from exercising lordship over the churches, did not control their charities. This is seen in Acts v. 4; xi. 29, 30; 1 Cor. xvi. 1, 2; 2 Cor. ix. 7. The churches, too, selected messengers to convey their charities.† Surely, if they chose those whom they put in charge of their pecuniary contributions, they appointed those to whom they committed their spiritual interests.

---

* See Acts xiii. 1–3; xiv. 26, 27.
† See 1 Cor. xvi. 3; 2 Cor. viii. 18, 19; Phil. ii. 25; iv. 18.

In view of all the considerations now presented, the position held by Baptists—namely, that the New-Testament churches appointed their officers—is established beyond successful denial. I term this the position of Baptists; for they alone hold it in the fulness of its significance. Certainly no other religious denomination in this country so holds it. There is among Episcopalians, Lutherans, Presbyterians, and Methodists no local church that has exclusive authority to appoint its minister or pastor. No rector is placed over an Episcopal congregation without the action of a bishop. With Lutherans, what is called the "Ministerium," which is "composed of ministers only," has the right of "licensing and ordaining ministers." Among Presbyterians, whatever a local church may do, the action of Presbytery is necessary in licensing and ordaining men to preach. With Methodists, pastors are settled over local churches by the appointment of bishops. Even the office of "local preacher" cannot be conferred by a local congregation. The action of a "Quarterly Conference" is necessary in granting license to preach.

Of these four large denominations it has to be said that their regulations with regard to the appointment of ministers are in conflict with the New-Testament principle of church independence. This principle is violated when a local church is denied the right of appointing its own officers. Congregationalists are generally supposed to agree with Baptists as to the appointment of ministers; but they do not. Their theory may be correct; but if so, their practice is a departure from it. They have what they call "Consociations" and "Associations," the former chiefly in Connecticut. With regard to these, Dr. Dexter admits that there are in them " Presbyterian tendencies ;" while of Associations he says: "As a matter of convenience, advantage has been taken of these regular assemblages of the pastors, by candidates for the pulpit, to present themselves, after thorough training, for examination for a certificate of approval—in common parlance, 'for licensure.'"*

It is easy to see that Dr. Dexter does not approve this method of "licensure;" but it is difficult to see how he can help it. The practice seems to be established.† In proof of this, I may quote from what *The Congregationalist* of April 13, 1881, says of the meeting of the Manhattan Association: "The principal business was the examination of four seniors of Union Seminary, who passed creditably and were licensed to preach." Among the examiners were Drs.

---

* Dexter *On Congregationalism*, p. 225, edition of 1865.

† To show the correctness of this view, I may state that Adoniram Judson was "licensed to preach" in the year 1810 by an "Association of Congregationalist Ministers." (See Wayland's *Memoir of Judson*, vol. i., p. 51.)

Wm. M. Taylor, R. S. Storrs, and Ray Palmer—quite renowned names. These distinguished men have thus given their sanction to the plan of licensing ministers, not by churches, but by Associations. Baptists stand alone in insisting that the right to license and ordain ministers is a right, under Christ, resident in a local church. It exists nowhere else. If exercised by bishops, Ministeriums, Consociations, or Associations, there is usurpation; and, of course, there is a violation of the order of the New Testament. Baptists believe that God calls men to preach the gospel, and that the churches recognize his call. They cannot make a minister, but they can approve what God has done—at least, what they believe he has done. This is all a church does in voting for the ordination of one of its members to the pastoral office. Believing him to be divinely called to the office, the church, by its vote, recognizes the call; and this vote of recognition is the essence of ordination. Such a vote must precede a Council of ordination, and the Council is called by the church of which the brother is a member. Andrew Fuller well remarks: "The only end for which I join in an ordination is to unite with the elders of that and other churches in *expressing my brotherly concurrence in the election, which, if it fell on what I accounted an unsound or unworthy character, I should withhold.* Though churches are so far independent of each other as that no one has a right to interfere in the concerns of another without their consent, unless it be as we all have a right to exhort and admonish one another, yet there is a common union required to subsist between them for the good of the whole; and, so far as the ordination of a pastor affects this common or general interest, it is fit that there should be a general concurrence in it. It was on this principle, I conceive, rather than as an exercise of authority, that the apostles, whose office was general, took the lead in the primitive ordinations. When the churches increased they appointed such men as Timothy and Titus to do what they would have done themselves had they been present; and when all extraordinary officers ceased, the same *general* object would be answered by the concurrence of the elders of the surrounding churches." *

No action of an ordaining Council can in any way impair the integrity or independence of the church which calls such Council. When a Council recognizes and approves what a church has done, its moral influence, though it can impart no grace, is promotive of the usefulness of the pastor ordained and of the church over which he presides. If, however, a Council should withhold its recognition and approval, and if, by its advice, the church should revoke its former

* Works of Andrew Fuller, vol. iii., p. 494.

action, there would be nothing in all this conflicting in the least with the doctrine of church independence.

SECTION VI.
Church action is final.

The independence of a church implies the right of a majority of its members to rule in accordance with the laws of Christ. In 2 Cor. ii. 6 it is written: "Sufficient to such a man is this punishment, which was inflicted of many." A literal translation of the words rendered "of many" would be "by the more" —that is, by the majority. The rendering of Macknight, and also of Davidson in his *Revision*, is "by the greater number." If, as has been shown, the governmental power of a church is with the members, it follows that a majority must rule—that is to say, either the majority or the minority must govern. But it is absurd to refer to the rule of the minority. That a majority must rule is so plain a principle of Independency, and so plain a principle of common sense, that it is needless to dwell upon it.

It has been stated on a preceding page that the power of a church cannot be transferred or alienated. From this fact results the finality of church action. The church at Corinth could not transfer her authority to the church at Philippi, nor could the church at Antioch convey her power to the church at Ephesus;

nor could all the apostolic churches delegate their power to an Association, a Synod, a Conference, or a Convention. The power of a church is manifestly inalienable, and, this being true, church action is final. That there is no tribunal higher than that of a church is evident from Matt. xviii. 15-17: "Moreover, if thy brother shall trespass against thee, go and tell him his fault between thee and him alone: If he shall hear thee, thou hast gained thy brother. But if he will not hear thee, then take with thee one or two more, that in the mouth of two or three witnesses every word may be established. And if he shall neglect to hear them, tell it unto the church; but if he neglect to hear the church, let him be unto thee as a heathen man and a publican."

Here the Saviour lays down a rule for the settlement of grievances among brethren. If the offender, when told of his fault, does not give satisfaction, the offended party is to take with him "one or two more, that in the mouth of two or three witnesses every word may be established." But if the offender "shall neglect to hear them," what is to be done? "Tell it to the church." What church? The aggregate body of the redeemed? This is equally impossible and absurd. I ask again, What church? Evidently the local congregation to which the parties belong. If the offender does not hear the church, what then and

DISTINCTIVE PRINCIPLES OF BAPTISTS. 207

finally? "Let him be unto thee as a heathen man and a publican"—that is, let the offender no longer be held in church-fellowship, but let him occupy the place of "a heathen man and a publican." There is to be an end to Christian fellowship and association. This idea cannot be more fully emphasized than by the reference to "a heathen man [a Gentile] and a publican," the most unworthy character, in Jewish estimation, to be found among Gentiles.

But can there be no appeal from the action of a single local church to an "Association" or a "Presbytery" or a "Conference"? No; there is no appeal. Shall an Association or a Presbytery or a Conference put the offender back in church-fellowship, when the church by its action classed him with heathens and publicans? This is too preposterous. What kind of fellowship would it be, when the church had declared the excluded member unworthy of its fellowship? Will it be asked, What is to be done if the action of a church does not give satisfaction to all concerned? I answer, Do what is done when the action of a Presbyterian General Assembly or a Methodist General Conference or an Episcopal General Convention does not give satisfaction. Do nothing. There must be a stopping-place; there must be final action. Baptists say, with the New Testament before them, that the action of each local congregation of baptized believers is final.* Let those who oppose the Baptist form of church government show anywhere in the Scriptures the remotest allusion to an appeal from the decision of a church to any other tribunal. It cannot be done. There were, in apostolic times, no tribunals analogous to modern Synods, Conferences, Conventions. Let those who affirm that there were such "courts of appeal" adduce the evidence. On them rests the burden of proof. Baptists deny that there is such proof, and say that for any man to furnish it is as difficult as for "a camel to go through the eye of a needle."

The view which I have presented of the independence of the first churches is in such full historical accordance with the facts in the case that many distinguished Pedobaptists have been obliged to concede it. They have done this while giving their practical sanction to other forms of church government. Hence Mosheim, a Lutheran and a bitter opponent of Baptists, in referring to the first century, says: "The

---

* The above reasoning takes it for granted that the excluded member is *justly* excluded. If so, he must give evidence of penitence, in order to his restoration. If *unjustly* excluded, and the church does not, when the injustice is shown, annul its action, the excluded member may apply for admission into a sister-church, which may, in the exercise of its independence, receive him without encroaching on the independence of the excluding church. The opposite view would imply that the excluding church has a monopoly of independence, which is absurd.

churches, in those early times, were entirely independent, none of them being subject to any foreign jurisdiction, but each governed by its own rulers and its own laws; for, though the churches founded by the apostles had this particular deference shown to them, that they were consulted in difficult and doubtful cases, yet they had no juridical authority, no sort of supremacy over the others, nor the least right to enact laws for them."*

Archbishop Whately, a dignitary of the Church of England, referring to the New-Testament churches, says: "They were each a distinct, independent community *on earth,* united by the common principles on which they were founded, and by their mutual agreement, affection, and respect, but not having any one recognized head on earth, or acknowledging any sovereignty of one of these societies over others." Again: "A CHURCH and a DIOCESE seem to have been for a considerable time *coextensive* and *identical.* And each church or diocese (and consequently each superintendent), though connected with the rest by ties of faith and hope and charity, seems to have been (as has been already observed) perfectly independent, as far as regards any power of control."†

This is strong testimony from a Lutheran and an

---

* Maclaine's *Mosheim,* Baltimore edition, vol. i., p. 39.
† *Kingdom of Christ,* Carter's edition, pp. 36, 44.

Episcopalian. They would have given a different account of the matter if they could have done so consistently with truth. They virtually condemned their denominational organizations in writing what I have quoted. I might refer to Neander, and to many other Pedobaptists of distinction who have expressed themselves in substance as Mosheim and Whately have done; but it is needless. Baptists are not dependent on the testimony of church historians. They make their appeal to the New Testament of our Lord and Saviour Jesus Christ. If all the church histories in the world said the monarchical or aristocratic form of church government was maintained from the death of the apostle John onward, they would not be moved by it while the New Testament represents every church as a democracy fully competent to transact its own business. "To the law and to the testimony;" "All scripture is given by inspiration of God, and is profitable for doctrine, for reproof, for correction, for instruction in righteousness: that the man of God may be perfect, thoroughly furnished unto all good works" (Isa. viii. 20; 2 Tim. iii. 16, 17).

Baptists have ever regarded every church as complete in itself, independent, so far as its government is concerned, of every other church under heaven. They have watched with jealous eye all encroachments on church independence. For their views on baptism—

its subjects and its act—a regenerated church-membership, and the independent form of church government, they have been persecuted, tortured, put to death. Their blood has flowed like water. From their ranks have been taken martyrs who, having endured " much tribulation," are now before the throne of God. But the principles of Baptists still live, and will live; for they are indestructible—divinely vital—cannot die.

SECTION VII.
Superior advantages of Independency.

If the form of church government advocated in this chapter is in accordance with the New Testament, it follows that it has advantages superior to those of all other forms of government. Some of these advantages will now be pointed out. Of church independence it may be said:

1. *It is best suited to every form of civil government.*

In monarchies, whether absolute or limited, there is no reason why the churches of Jesus Christ should not be independent. Monarchies have to do with men as civil subjects, but not in their relations to God. The power of the monarch is a secular power, and cannot be rightfully exercised outside of the realm of secular jurisdiction; while Christianity belongs to the spiritual realm and confines itself to it. But even when monarchy transcends its proper limits and interferes with spiritual concerns, there is no reason why the independent form of church government should be exchanged for any other. In proof of this I need only refer to the fact that the apostolic churches were independent while the tyrant Nero reigned at Rome and caused the weight of his sceptre to be felt in all the provinces of his empire. The churches even then, wherever permitted to meet for worship, transacted whatever business claimed their attention.

What has been said of monarchies may, of course, be said with greater emphasis of aristocratic forms of civil government. Under the legitimate operation of such governments there is no encroachment on the rights of churches, and the doctrine of church independence can be exemplified without collision with the civil authority.

What is true of monarchies and aristocracies may be said with supreme emphasis of republics; for the latter recognize the people as the source of governmental power. This recognition accords with the philosophy of independent church government. If in monarchies, where the people are supposed to exist for the purpose of carrying into effect the monarch's will; if in aristocracies, where the people are reduced, comparatively, to ciphers—churches can flourish in their independence, much more is this independence cherished under the auspices of republican government. Truly, then, may it be said that church independence is best suited to every form of civil government.

2. *It is in accord with the tendencies of the age.*

The most superficial observer of men and things is aware that the democratic element has—occasionally, at least—indicated its existence in Europe for some centuries, while in recent years it has increased in strength. The colloquial remark has been attributed to Thomas Jefferson—whether truly or not I cannot say—that "the former European doctrine was that the great mass of men were born with saddles on their backs, while a few were born with boots and spurs on, and that the purpose of Divine Providence was for those with the boots and spurs to ride those having the saddles on them."

If this absurd doctrine has not been exploded, it is certainly in a process of explosion. Oppressed humanity, under the burdens imposed by monarchy and aristocracy, is everywhere restless and waiting for a suitable opportunity to assert its rights. The tendencies of the age are in favor of bringing the democratic element out of obscurity and exalting it to prominence. It is fast becoming an axiom that the people are the source of power, and that sovereignty inheres in them—not in kings and aristocracies, but in the people. How much the practical workings of church independence have had to do in developing the doctrine of popular rights it is impossible to say, but there is every reason to believe that they have promoted the development. Hence it may be said without hesitation that church independence is in accord with the tendencies of the age.

3. *It gives suitable prominence to the membership of a church.*

This is seen in the fact that without the agency of a church nothing can be done. Pastor and deacons are powerless if a church declines to act. Their *official* business is to do that for which they are elected by the suffrages of the church of which they are members. They are responsible, under Christ, to the church from which they receive not only *official* authority, but *official* existence. In the forms of government preferred by Episcopalians, Lutherans, Presbyterians, and Methodists there is only an indirect recognition of the body of the members as the source of power. The recognition is more decided among Presbyterians than among the rest, but it is not complete. The constitution of their "highest court," the General Assembly, is proof of this. The tribunal of last appeal is composed of ministers and ruling elders in equal numbers. This equality indicates a very partial concession of rights to the members. Every one can see this who will take the trouble to learn how much greater is the number of members than of ministers. With regard to Episcopalians, it will be seen how powerless the members are, even in connection with the "inferior clergy," when it is stated that in their General Conventions nothing can be done without the concurrence of the "House of Bishops." That the people are comparatively ignored by Lutheranism appears in the fact that a "Ministerium," that "licenses ministers," is composed entirely of ministers, and that the Synod, the highest tribunal, from which there is no appeal, is formed by an equal number of "clerical and lay delegates." Among Methodists the "lay element" is conspicuous by its absence. Within the memory of many persons now living it was entirely absent; for Annual and General Conferences were made up exclusively of "preachers." In some sections of the country this rigid rule is now somewhat relaxed, but how meagre is "lay representation" in any Conference! In opposition to all these aristocratic forms of church government, and in practical condemnation of them all, the independent form presents itself, inviting examination and challenging admiration for what it does in giving suitable prominence to the members of a church. They are not ciphers, but the depositaries of the governmental power that Christ has conferred. Independency accepts this fact and claims it as one of its superior advantages.

4. *Another advantage is seen in the appointment of church officers.*

These officers are of two classes—pastors and deacons. The former are in special charge of the spiritualities, and the latter of the temporalities, of the churches. Who can be so competent to choose these officers as the churches themselves? With the scriptural qualifications for the two offices as given by inspired men, cannot the churches best decide who among them should fill those offices? Can they not tell who are men of such Christian integrity and sanctified common sense as will most probably, if not most certainly, "use the office of a deacon well"? So also as to pastors. These are to "watch for souls as they that must give account," and who are so well qualified to select the men to preside as the churches to be presided over? Shall they not decide who shall watch for their souls and for the souls of the impenitent around them? Are they not best prepared to say who among them possess the moral and the spiritual requisites, as enumerated by Paul, for the office of bishop? As to the intellectual qualification implied in the words "apt to teach," who can so satisfactorily tell that a man is apt to teach as those who have been taught by him? The independence of the churches, as illustrated in the appointment of their officers, must commend itself to the common sense of all unprejudiced persons. The ad-

DISTINCTIVE PRINCIPLES OF BAPTISTS. 217

vantage of this form of government over every other must be apparent. The great thing, however, to be said for it is that it accords with the New Testament.

5. *It furnishes the most effectual preservative from doctrinal error.*

Doubtless many persons will at once dissent from this view. They suppose that a consolidated church, embracing a province or a kingdom, is the best protection from the inroads of heresy. They think that the very compactness of such a church must resist the subtle influences of error, however penetrating those influences may be. Is this so? Has it been historically true? Was it true of the Church of England when Lord Chatham said that it had "a Calvinistic creed, a Popish liturgy, and an Arminian clergy"? Is it true now, when various false doctrines receive not only toleration, but encouragement, and when the mere existence of what are termed "Broad Church" views implies that the very foundations of orthodoxy are disturbed? No; the Church of England with its "Thirty-Nine Articles," more than three centuries old, is vulnerable to the assaults of false doctrine. Its strong ecclesiastic bands, riveted by Parliamentary enactments, create a compactness which gives greater facility to the infectious diffusion of error. "A little leaven leaveneth the whole lump." This is true whether the lump be large or small; but the danger is greater where there is one large mass than where there are many that are small. Far be it from me to say that a church with the independent form of government may not become corrupted by heretical doctrines. History would falsify such a statement; but the corruption of one such church would have no necessary connection with the corruption of another. Indeed, the very independence of the churches might be, and if they were in a proper spiritual state would be, utilized in preventing the spread of the doctrinal corruption. On the other hand, a consolidated church, coextensive with a state or a kingdom, would furnish few if any facilities for arresting the tide of error when once set in. A local church, under a sense of its responsibility, is quick to detect the first appearance of vital heresy and to stamp it with censure. If the heretic sees his error, confesses it, and renounces it, the evil is at an end; if he persists in it, the church withdraws its fellowship from him and he becomes comparatively powerless for mischief. Suppose such a heretical minister to belong to the Presbyterian Church. He first disturbs the local congregation, then the Presbytery, then the Synod, and finally the General Assembly. Thus he has one opportunity after another to make known and to defend his false doctrines; so that the Presbyterian form of government, instead of preserving from doctrinal heresy, may, in the sense

DISTINCTIVE PRINCIPLES OF BAPTISTS. 219

indicated, promote it. Who does not see that church independence is the best preservative from doctrinal error? Dr. Hodge is said to have expressed his wonder at the uniformity among Baptist ministers as to matters of doctrine, in view of the independence of Baptist churches. Perhaps his philosophical mind overlooked the fact that the uniformity is promoted by the independence.

I have referred to the withdrawal of fellowship on the part of a church from a heretic as a means of arresting the spread of doctrinal error. Another thing deserves mention: Where an entire church becomes heretical in doctrine or disorderly in practice, other churches, in the exercise of their independence, may withdraw their fellowship from it, and thus confine its injurious influence to its own narrow limits. Whether, therefore, we consider doctrinal error in connection with an individual church-member or in connection with a church itself, the independent form of government is the best security against its contagious encroachments.

Nor is this all.

6. *It secures, also, more satisfactory corrective discipline.*

There is no perfection in this world. It may be sought more hopefully among the churches of the saints than elsewhere, but even there it will be sought in vain. All that is said in the New Testament about corrective church discipline implies the imperfection of church-members. This imperfection often shows itself in greater or less degrees. In its ordinary manifestations it must be borne with. Christian love and Christian forbearance require this. Sometimes, however, a church-member so violates his Christian obligations as to grieve his brethren, who admonish him and labor in the spirit of meekness to restore him. Ordinarily, they are successful and the offending brother is happily reclaimed. This is not always the case; in some instances it becomes the duty of a church to pass an act of exclusion. This, as we have seen, the New Testament not only authorizes, but requires. In a case of this kind the offender is arraigned and the charge or charges, with distinct specifications, are presented. The church sits as a Christian jury and hears all the testimony in the case. The arraigned brother has every opportunity to explain and rebut, if possible, the testimony against him. The church is disposed to give him the benefit of all doubts, but after a full hearing of the matter is convinced that the glory of God and the honor of his cause demand the exclusion of the brother. He is therefore excluded. The act of exclusion may offend him and not satisfy his kindred and partisan friends; but is it practicable to administer corrective discipline so satisfactorily in any other way? The man has been tried by his peers and found guilty. These peers, too, are of the "vicinage," and fully competent to understand and appreciate all local circumstances bearing on the case. Does not the civil law mean something in providing for "a jury of the vicinage"? There is profound significance in the independence of each church, so far as the trial and the exclusion of a guilty member may be concerned. While, therefore, it cannot be said that the independent form of church government secures an absolutely satisfactory corrective church discipline, it may be said that the discipline so provided for is the most satisfactory that can be had.

7. *It cherishes a sense of individual responsibility.*

This is a matter of great importance, for Christianity is an intensely personal thing. It has to do with men in their individual relations to God. There is no such thing as the regeneration of *masses* of men, nor is there regeneration by proxy. The great change takes place in the individual heart. Nothing is more personal than regeneration. When the materials of a Christian church are reduced to units, the units are found in regenerated persons. There is personal repentance, personal faith, personal baptism. In making a profession of Christianity, personal obligations are recognized and publicly assumed. Church relations do not impair, but intensify, a sense of individual responsibility. An impressive consciousness of this fact is indispensable to a proper performance of church duties.

To show that the independent form of church government cherishes a sense of individual responsibility, it is sufficient to say that all matters coming before a church are decided by the votes of the members. They vote as individuals; and, as a majority rules, no one can tell but his vote may be decisive. Surely, then, every vote should be intelligently given; and this view of the case is a strong argument in favor of sanctified intelligence. Questions of great importance must be decided. These questions not only involve the spiritual welfare of the church itself, but often have an important bearing on the local interests of the community and the general interests of the kingdom of Christ. Church-officers are chosen by the suffrages of the members. How essential that the right man be appointed as pastor! In order to this, church-members must be acquainted with the purity of his Christian character, and also with his doctrinal soundness. A vote referring to two points so vital as these must be given under a sense of responsibility. The influence of deacons has much to do with the condition of a church, and therefore the best men should be appointed to the office. A church too must decide what objects of Christian work should receive its encouragement and patronage. These objects may be so numerous that all of them cannot receive attention, and if so, there must be a selection of those deemed most important. What shall be the proportion of pecuniary aid given to Home Missions, Foreign Missions, Publication Work, and Ministerial Education, the church must decide. The decision is no trivial matter. It calls for a union of knowledge and piety.

One of the most painful duties of a church is to deal in a way of discipline with unworthy members. In all the proceedings in such cases the laws of Christ are to be sacredly observed. These laws, then, must be understood that they may be intelligently applied. A member who is guilty of "disorderly conduct," and who fails to give satisfaction by penitence and reformation, must be excluded. It is a solemn thing to withdraw the hand of fellowship, and it must be done under a sense of responsibility. When, according to apostolic command, "a heretic" is to be "rejected," the act of rejection is to be performed by the church. A renunciation of the fundamental doctrines of the gospel demands this step. As a general thing, the members of a local church, having been regenerated by the Holy Spirit and justified by faith in Jesus Christ, are competent judges of sound doctrine. They may not understand many theological niceties, but they know the way of salvation. They "have an unction from the Holy One" (1 John ii. 20).

In view of all these considerations, showing what obligations rest on church-members and what duties are required at their hands, I affirm with strongest emphasis that the independent form of government cherishes a sense of individual responsibility. Those who have to decide great questions by their votes are in a responsible position. This fact impresses them; they cannot ignore it; they would not if they could. Their responsibility as church-members is to the Head of the church—the Lord Jesus Christ—and it is stamped with all the sacredness of the blood of his atoning sacrifice. Let the church-member take his stand by the cross, remembering that he has been individually redeemed by him who died thereon, and he will cherish a sense of individual responsibility. He will feel the weight of the personal obligations resting on him. The doctrine of church independency will deepen his consciousness of these obligations; for it will teach him that he is not a *cipher*, but a *man*—A REDEEMED MAN, and ere long to be A GLORIFIED MAN.

CONCLUSION.

The foregoing pages show that there is something distinctive in the principles of Baptists. They differ from all other denominations; and the difference is so great as not only to justify, but to demand, their separate existence as a people. They are God's witnesses, and they are his only witnesses who "tell the truth, the whole truth, and nothing but the truth," on the points referred to in this volume. Should their testimony be suppressed, in what religious denomination could "the whole truth" concerning the subjects of baptism be found? Not one. The question, Who should be baptized? would receive an answer in positive conflict with the teachings of the New Testament. Who but Baptists declare "the whole truth" with regard to the exclusive baptismal act and the symbolic import of the act? If there are others, where are they? We know not. Nor do we know of any people, besides Baptists, who maintain "the whole truth" on the subject of a regenerated church-membership, embracing, as it does, the vital point that we come to the church through Christ, and not to Christ through the church and its ordinances. Baptists proclaim in the audience of the whole world that persons have nothing to do with church relations and gospel ordinances *till they are regenerated*. Among whom, except Baptists, is the doctrine of church independency fully exemplified? Throughout this broad land we look in vain for the exemplification. Truly, Baptists are important witnesses; for they testify important things, and theirs is the only testimony on these important matters.

In view of the facts to which attention has been called in this volume, there are certain duties incumbent on Baptists, such as the following:

1. *They should acquaint themselves more thoroughly with Baptist principles.*

The *Baptist Year-Book* for 1882 reports more than two and a third millions of Baptists in the United States. This is a large number, but it is sad to think that there may be in it many persons who cannot give a satisfactory reason why they are Baptists. Honesty and veracity would possibly require some to say, "We are Baptists because our fathers and mothers were." Some might have to say, "The Baptists were the leading people where we made profession of religion, and we joined them." Others, in telling the truth of the matter, might be obliged to say, "We became Christians in time of revival, and, as most of the converts united with the Baptists, we did so too." Others still would possibly find a suitable representative in the brother who said, "I liked the Baptist minister better than any other, and wished to be a member of his church."

What reasons are these for being Baptists! It is not necessary to say that such reasons should have no influence, but they certainly should not be decisive. Proper reasons for becoming Baptists are to be found in the New Testament. They will be found without

DISTINCTIVE PRINCIPLES OF BAPTISTS. 227

being specially sought—that is to say, if the New Testament is faithfully and diligently studied, the principles which distinguish Baptists will be discovered. That these principles are in accordance with, and the outgrowth of, the teachings of Christ and the apostles is the conclusive reason why any one should be a Baptist. Let these principles be understood and appreciated, and there will be *decided* Baptists. They will be Baptists because they can be nothing else. The plain teachings of Scripture will permit them to be nothing else. It is "a lamentation, and shall be for a lamentation," that any Baptists should have only a superficial acquaintance with the principles they profess. Such persons, whether few or many, need instruction that they may be intelligent Baptists, and that they may be able to give to every one who asks them a reason for their faith and practice.

2. *Baptists should be more zealous in the propagation of their principles.*

Good principles are good things, but they have no self-propagating power. Principles are powerless apart from the persons who hold them. Baptists sometimes forget this. They are so confident of the correctness of their principles as to feel that all will be well. They think that their views, without any effort on their part, will commend themselves to general acceptance. They suppose that a good cause may be left to take care of itself; but no cause, however good, takes care of itself. Its friends must advocate it, and by their advocacy secure its triumph. Baptists must not forget that they are "fellow-helpers to the truth." None of them should fail to give the "truth" their help. None should ever act as if they were ashamed of being Baptists. Their principles, when assailed, should never lack defence or vindication from them. Their silence, when they should speak, would be a culpable and an injurious silence. Baptists should be ready not only to meet and to repel attacks made on their principles, but should earnestly engage in the propagation of those principles. Leaving, on suitable occasions, their fortresses of defence, they should invade the domain of error and become actively aggressive. This is one fault of some of the Baptists of this generation—that they do not zealously propagate their distinctive views. They should see to it that the truth as embodied in their distinctive principles is brought into direct, positive, constant, exterminating contact with the error opposed to those principles. What distinctive mission have Baptists, if this is not their mission?—to present the truth in love on the matters wherein they differ from Pedobaptists. What is there but this that justifies their denominational existence and saves them from the reproach of being schismatics? If they have a right to denominational life, it is their duty to propagate their distinctive principles, without which that life cannot be maintained.

3. *They should pray more earnestly for the success and triumph of their distinctive principles.*

It is supposed by many that controversy drives away the spirit of prayer. Were this so, it would be very sad; for there would be no spirit of prayer. Controversy is a necessity, and will be so long as truth and error are in the world. There may not at all times be controversy going on in the *technical* sense, but really and truly there is always controversy when truth and error are in collision. God is on the side of truth. Baptists worthy of the name believe without a doubt that their distinctive principles are true. Hence they can in all good conscience appeal to God in prayer, and ask him to care for his own truth and vindicate it by giving it success. Active effort to inculcate and diffuse the truth should ever be preceded, accompanied, and followed by prayer. No principle is worth holding, the success and triumph of which cannot be consistently prayed for. Baptists, above all persons, should pray. Other denominations that capture infants in their cradles and claim them as "the baptized children of the church" are not so dependent on God for the continuance of their ecclesiastical life as are Baptists. For the latter there is no hope but in God—no hope, unless he by his Spirit regenerates individuals of accountable years and thus fits them for membership in the churches. While Baptists must never fail to use means to disseminate their distinctive principles, they must call earnestly on God in prayer to give to those principles the success and triumph to which their importance and their value entitle them. There is wonderful efficacy in prayer. Let Baptists test its efficacy in connection with their distinctive principles.

I present only one point more:

4. *Pedobaptists should candidly examine the distinctive principles of Baptists.*

These principles are not understood by multitudes in Pedobaptist communities. It is supposed that immersion as baptism is the only thing specially characteristic of Baptists. Nor is this view confined to persons of ordinary intelligence. I have it from a perfectly credible source that General R. E. Lee not many years before his death said that he had just heard concerning the Baptists what surprised him—namely, that they did not baptize infants! If General Lee had not known this all his life, what is to be said of persons of inferior intelligence? The General was an Episcopalian. Pedobaptists should inform themselves as to what Baptists believe. It would do them good, for it would give them important ideas on the subject of scriptural churches and Christian ordinances. Many of them, too, would be led to make a personal profession of their faith in the act of Christian immersion. It was an examination of Baptist principles that influenced Adoniram Judson, Luther Rice, Horatio B. Hackett, Alexander Carson, Baptist W. Noel, N. M. Crawford, D. R. Campbell, Richard Fuller, and many others, to renounce the errors of Pedobaptism, and to illustrate the spirit of obedience to Christ by being "buried with him in baptism."

INDEX.

A.

ABRAHAM, 14, 19, 31, 38, 48, 49, 50, 51, 52.
   justified by faith before circumcision, 56.
   lineal descent from, no claim, 60.
Allen, John, 99.
Aristobulus, 108.
Aristotle, 106.
Astolphus, 142.
Augsburg Confession, 161.
Augusti, 139.
Augustine, 78.
Austin, monk, 150.

B.

Baptism, administration of, in New Testament, 121.
   a figure, 54.
   Apostolic Epistles on, 33–39.
   argument for more than one, 155.
   circumcision and, 63–72.
   classical use of word, 104–109.
   defined by Peter, 35.
   derivation of word, 90–96.
   design of, 113–121.
   historical record of, 135–146.
   infant, 16.
      effect on Christ's ordinance, 87.

Baptism, infant, effect on church, 82.
   effect on subjects, 84–87.
   no good reason for, 80.
   supposed reference to, in Old Testament, 30–33.
   John's, 13, 14, 121–123.
   meaning of word, 96–104.
   not a seal, 54.
   not administered by Christ, 15.
   of Christ not initiation to priestly office, 123.
   of Ethiopian eunuch, 24.
   of Saul, 151.
   Pedobaptist objection to, 147–158.
   prerequisites to, 159–168.
   use of word in New Testament, 110–112.
   Westminster Confession on, 38.
Baptismal regeneration, 160.
Baptisms, household, 25–29.
Baptist Year Book, 226.
Baptists as witnesses to the truth, 225.
   in what they agree with other denominations, 11.
Barnes, Rev. Albert, 33, 119, 190, 199.
Baxter, Richard, 135.
Beecher, Dr. Edward, 109, 112.
Beza, 198.

Bishop, meaning of, 183.
    of London, 91.
Blackstone, 96.
Bloomfield, 119.
Booth, 136 (note).
Boswell, 136 (note).
Brewster, Sir David, 142.
Brown, Dr. J. Newton, 164, 165.

C.

Calvin, John, 81, 99, 100, 103, 133, 140, 143, 157.
Campbell, Alexander, 41, 126.
Campbell, Dr. D. R., 230.
Campbell, Dr. George, 100, 103.
Carson, Dr. Alexander, 105, 230.
Chalmers, Dr. Thomas, 101, 115, 119.
Chatham, Lord, 217.
Chillingworth, 80.
Church, difference between so-called "Jewish" and Christian, 44.
Church, a, 42–44.
    authority over members, 190–195.
    Baptist understanding of, 169–174.
    independence of, 182–224.
    officers of, 195.
Circumcision, 53–72.
    of Timothy, 67.
Clarke, Dr. Adam, 118, 119, 122 (note).
Coleman, Dr. Lyman, 198.
Commission, the Great, 17–21.
Conant, Dr. T. J., 32, 105.
Constitution of the United States, 19.
Consubstantiation, 175, 181.
Corinth, church at, 28, 31.
Cornelius, 25.
Council of Carthage, 76.

Council of Jerusalem, 69, 199.
    of Ravenna, 143.
    of Trent, 82.
Covenant of Christian Church, 49.
    of so-called Jewish Church, 50.
Crawford, Dr. N. M., 230.
Cressy, the monks of, 143.
Crispus, 28.
Cummins, Bishop, 163.
Cyprian, 77, 78.

D.

Daniel, 45,
Davidson, Dr., 32, 35, 205.
Deacons, 196.
Dexter, Dr., 202.
Diodati, 198.
Diodorus Siculus, 106.
Doddridge, Dr., 73, 110, 119.
Duncan, W. C., D. D., 95 (note).

E.

Edward VI., 143, 144.
Elizabeth, Queen, 140, 144.
Erasmus, 75, 76, 198.
Ernesti, 110.
Ethiopian eunuch, baptism of, 24, 129.

F.

Fidus, 77.
Fonts, use of, 141.
Fuller, Andrew, 204 (note).
Fuller, J. G., 172 (note).
Fuller, Dr. Richard, 230.

G.

Greek prepositions, 130, 147.
Gregory the Great, Pope, 150.
Griffin, Dr. E. D., 172.

H.

Hackett, Dr. Horatio B., 230.

INDEX.

Hagar a type of the so-called Jewish Church, 58.
Harrison on Greek prepositions, 147.
Henry, 81.
Heraclides Ponticus, 106.
Herod, 108, 126.
Hibbard, Dr., 39, 41, 47.
Hippocrates, 106.
Hodge, Dr. Charles, 41, 42, 50, 53, 64, 111, 161, 219.
Household baptism among Karens in Burmah, 29.

I.

Irenæus, 72, 73, 74, 79.

J.

Jailer, the, of Philippi, 27.
James I., 148.
    his rules to translators, 91.
Jefferson, Thomas, 213.
Jerome, or Hierom, 75.
Jewish Church, so-called, 39.
John the Baptist, 13, 15, 16, 44, 46, 47, 124, 148,
Johnson, Samuel, 97, 136.
Josephus, 107.
Judd, Rev. Willard, 137, 138 (note).
Judson, Adoniram, 202 (note), 230.

K.

Krauth, Dr., 162.
Knox, John, 143.

L.

Lee, General R. E., 230.
Liddell & Scott, 94, 95.
Lightfoot, Dr., 122.
Lord's Supper, observance of, 174–182.
Lucian, 108, 109.

Luther, Martin, 81.
Lydia, 25–27.

M.

Maclaine, 137 (note).
Macknight, Dr., 119, 155, 205,
Mary, Queen, 140, 143.
Melanchthon, 161.
Miller, Dr. Samuel, 40, 63, 65, 81, 124, 125, 126, 127, 137.
Milton, 97.
Monica, 78.
Moses, law to, cannot affect the Saviour's command, 38.
Mosheim, 137, 208, 210.

N.

Neander, 37, 77, 78, 137, 138, 210.
Nebuchadnezzar's dream, 45.
Nero, 212.
Newton, Dr. Richard, 163, 164.
Noah, 19.
Noel, Rev. Baptist W., 230.
North British Review, 71.
Noyes, Dr., 32.

O.

Old Testament, no authority for infant baptism in, 38.
Old Version of Scriptures, 91.
Origen, 74, 75, 76.

P.

Palmer, Dr. Ray, 203.
Paul on baptism, 14, 26, 28, 30, 33, 35, 37.
    on the covenants, 50, 51, 52, 56.
Peck, J. M., D. D., 187.
Pentecost, no infant baptism on the day of, 21.
Pepin, 142.
Peter, 22, 23, 25, 35, 54.

Philip, 24, 129.
Pindar, 105, 106, 109.
Plutarch, 108.
Pringle, Rev. William, 133.

R.

Regeneration, 12.
  baptismal, 160, 164.
Rice, Dr. Luther, 230.
Rice, Dr. N. L., 41, 64, 126, 149.
Ripley, Dr., H. J., 172 (note).
Robinson, Dr. Edward, 121, 149.
Rufinus, 75, 76.

S.

Sarah, type of the Christian Church, 58.
Saul of Tarsus, baptism of, 151.
Silas, 27,
Stanley, Dean, 102, 144, 145, 157.
Stephanas, 28, 37.
Stephen II., Pope, 142, 143.
Stuart, Professor Moses, 37, 93, 102, 104, 105, 108, 139.
Storrs, Dr. R. S., 203.
Strabo, 107.

Summers, Dr. Thomas O., 49, 50, 53, 64, 81, 130, 131.

T.

Taylor, Dr. William M., 203.
Tertullian, 74, 100.
Timon, 108.
Transubstantiation, 175, 181.
Tyndale, William, 116, 197.

W.

Wall, Dr., 37, 72, 73, 74, 75, 76, 79, 93, 119, 140, 141.
Walker, Mr., 140.
Watson, Richard, 111 (note), 112, 156, 157.
Webster, Daniel, 60, 97.
Wesley, John, 81, 119, 136.
Westminster Confession, 38.
Whately, Archbishop, 209, **210**.
Whitby, Dr., 93.
Whitefield, 119.
Winer, 73.
Woods, Dr., 37.
Worcester, 97.

INDEX OF SCRIPTURES.

GENESIS.
	PAGE
3 : 15	51
12 : 3	52
17	52
17 : 11	53
22 : 18	52

NUMBERS.
31 : 23	155

2 KINGS.
4	77

PSALMS.
77 : 17	154

PROVERBS.
8 : 4	23

ISAIAH.
2 : 2	44
8 : 20	210

JEREMIAH.
31 : 31–34	56

DANIEL.
2 : 44	45

MATTHEW.
2 : 11–14, 20–22	130
3 : 2	46
3 : 9	60
3 : 11	100
5 : 19	13
8 : 31–33	131
9 : 17	131
16 : 18	45
18 : 15–17	206
18 : 17	193
19 : 13	16
21 : 43	30
23 : 13	49
25 : 46	131
27 : 25	61
28 : 18, 19, 20	78
33 : 21	13, 189

MARK.
1 : 15	46
9 : 22	131
16 : 15, 16	18

LUKE.
1 : 39	151
12 : 50	110
15 : 18	151
15 : 20	152
16 : 16	46
24 : 46, 47	18

JOHN.
1 : 11	30

Reference	Page
3 : 7	48
3 : 22, 23	133
3 : 23	124, 127
3 : 26 ; 4 : 1, 2	15
4 : 1	48

ACTS.

Reference	Page
1 : 3	189
2 : 38	117
2 : 38, 39	22
2 : 41	23
2 : 47	61
5 : 4	200
6	196
7 : 38	41, 43, 44
8 : 38	122, 133
8 : 38, 39	129
9 : 18	151, 152
9 : 39	152
10 : 47	152
11 : 22	200
11 : 29, 30	200
13 : 1–3	200 (note)
14 : 23	197
14 : 26, 27	200 (note)
15	69, 199
16	27
16 : 13, 14, 15	25
16 : 30–34	153
18 : 8	28
19 : 4	14
19 : 32, 41	42
20 : 28	183
21 : 17–25	70
22 : 16	117

ROMANS.

Reference	Page
1 : 7	190
4 : 2	56
4 : 11	53
6	136
6 : 2, 3	34
6 : 3, 4, 5	114
6 : 3–7	115
6 : 4	138, 152
10 : 17	24
11	30
11 : 19, 20	31
14 : 1	190

1 CORINTHIANS.

Reference	Page
1 : 16	28
1 : 24	23
5 : 1–5	191
7 : 14	31
10 : 2	155
10 : 17	181
11 : 26	181
11 : 20–34	175
15 : 3, 4	114
15 : 29	34, 118
16 : 1, 2	200
16 : 3	200 (note)
16 : 15	28

2 CORINTHIANS.

Reference	Page
2 : 6	205
2 : 6–8	193
8 : 18, 19	200 (note)
8 : 19	198
9 : 7	200
15 : 29	118

GALATIANS.

Reference	Page
3 : 7, 29	56
3 : 14	31
3 : 16	52
3 : 17	51
3 : 27	34
4 : 22–31	58
5 : 2	71
5 : 12	192

INDEX OF SCRIPTURES.

EPHESIANS.

	PAGE
1 : 13	54
2 : 15	62
4 : 5	113
4 : 30	54

PHILIPPIANS.

2 : 25; 4 : 18..............200 (note)

COLOSSIANS.

2	136
2 : 12	34, 114, 138

2 THESSALONIANS.

3 : 6..................191, 193

1 TIMOTHY.

6 : 12..................34

2 TIMOTHY.

	PAGE
3 : 16, 17	210

HEBREWS.

1 : 1, 2	45
8 : 6	57
8 : 8–12	56
8 : 9	55
9 : 10	155
10 : 22	35

1 PETER.

3 : 21..................35, 114

1 JOHN.

2 : 20..................223

THE END.

A Biographical Sketch of James Madison Pendleton (1811-1891)

By

John Franklin Jones

A Biographical Sketch of James Madison Pendleton (1811-1891)

James Madison Pendleton–pastor, educator, professor, theologian, author, editor--was named for President Madison (*ESB*). He was born November 20, 1811 in Spottsylvania County, Virginia, to John and Frances J. (Cathcart) Thompson Pendleton, who were married in 1806 (*ESB*). The family moved to Christian County, Kentucky when he was one year old, settling on a farm near Pembroke. He lived there until age twenty, attending the best available schools during the winter months (Cathcart).

The young Pendleton, though interested in religion at fifteen, was converted at seventeen. He united with the Bethel church, near Pembroke, being baptized April 14, 1829 by Rev. John S. Wilson (Cathcart).

He was licensed to preach in February 1831, the only licentiate of the Bethel church prior to 1878. He entered the Christian County Seminary, Hopkinsville, in 1833, at which he pursued a course of study in the Latin and Greek classics. Simultaneously with his schooling, he preached alternate Sundays at the Hopkinsville and Bethel churches. The Hopkinsville church ordained him November 1, 1833 (Cathcart). Pendleton has the distinction of being the first man in southern Kentucky who gave himself wholly to the full-time ministry (*ESB*).

He moved to the church in Bowling Green, Kentucky, in

1837, where he served for twenty years (Cathcart). In 1852 and upon Pendleton's invitation, James Robinson Graves came to Bowling Green and conducted a revival. Pendleton endorsed Graves' views on alien immersion and nonpulpit affiliation. Upon Graves' insistence, Pendleton wrote an exposition of those views. Graves published the views as *An Old Landmark Re-set*, the magnum opus of Landmarkism. Pendleton was closely associated with Graves and gained a reputation as the theologian of Landmarkism (*ESB*).

Pendleton espoused Henry Clay's gradual emancipation measures in 1849 and supported them via many newspaper articles. Notwithstanding the dispersion of his views, Kentucky voted against the measures, and slavery remained unchanged until overthrown by the Civil War (Cathcart).

He was elected Professor of Theology at Union University, Murfreesborough, Tennessee January 1, 1857. Joseph H. Eaton was then president of that institution (*ESB*). Pendleton took the position upon the proviso that he continue his preaching and pastorates. Thereupon, he immediately assumed the pastorate at the Baptist church in Murfreesborough (Cathcart).

In 1858, he became joint editor, along with Amos Cooper Dayton, of the *Tennessee Baptist*, of which J. R. Graves had been long-time editor (*ESB*).

Pendleton's father advocated abolition (*ESB*). The Civil War and the younger Pendleton's loyalty to the Union necessitated his removal to Hamilton, Ohio, where he resided between 1862 and 1865. In November 1865, he moved to his last pastoral position, the Upland Baptist Church, Upland, Pennsylvania (Cathcart). While serving there, Pendleton helped establish Crozer Theological Seminary (*ESB*).

He resigned the Upland church due to age and returned to Nashville, Tennessee in June 1883. Mrs. Pendleton became blind due to cataracts. Pendleton divided the remainder of his days among his children. He died at Bowling Green,

Kentucky March 5, 1891. The funeral service was conducted by T. T. Eaton of Louisville in the Baptist church at Bowling Green, and Pendleton was buried in Fairview Cemetery there (*ESB*).

Pendleton wrote prolifically for his denomination and the local, community papers of his residences. He published many pamphlets, tracts, and sermons. Among them are *Thoughts on Christian Duty* (1851); *Three Reasons Why I Am a Baptist* (1853); *An Old Landmark Re-set* (1856); and *Church Manual* (1867) (Cathcart).

His *Christian Doctrines, a Compendium of Theology* (1878) is masterly, concise, logical, orthodox, and comprehensive (Cathcart). (This volume was the textbook for the first theology formally studied by this writer.)

He penned *Christianity Susceptible of Legal Proof* (1876). With George W. Clark, he co- authored *Brief Notes on the New Testament* (1883). He wrote *The Atonement of Christ* (1884-85) while spending the winter in Austin, Texas. He wrote *Notes on Sermons* in Bowling Green, Kentucky. He began writing *Reminiscences of a Long Life* on his 79th birthday in 1890 and completed it in two months (*ESB*).

The theologian was an avid student. He devoted his mornings exclusively to study and his afternoons to pastoral work. Cathcart said of him:

> He is devout, serious, conscientious, and yet highly appreciates good wit and humor, and is ready and judicious in the use of them. He is of medium height, well proportioned, firm of step as of convictions, a sincere friend, generous to every good cause according to his ability, unostentatious and affable with his friends, reserved among strangers, and cautious of his associations. His integrity of character and honesty of conviction are absolutely above suspicion, and are due to his abiding, unshaken trust in God (Cathcart, 897-98).

A Biographical Sketch of James Madison Pendleton

On March 18, 1838, shortly after moving to Bowling Green, he married Catherine S. Garnett of Glasgow, Kentucky. Their first child, Letitia, was born January 8, 1839. John Malcolm, born May 5, 1840, later joined the Confederate army and was killed in the Civil War. Fannie was born March 11, 1844. She married Leslie Waggener in 1867. Waggener became president of Bethel College in Russellville, Kentucky, a college Pendleton helped to establish in 1849. Lila, a third daughter, was born August 25, 1850 while he was pastor at Russellville. Garnett, their last child, was born in Bowling Green, May 24, 1855 (*ESB*).

BIBLIOGRAPHY

Cathcart, William, ed. *The Baptist Encyclopaedia: A Dictionary of the Doctrines, Ordinances, Usages, Confessions of Faith, Sufferings, Labors, and Successes, and of the General History of the Baptist Denomination in All Lands, with Numerous Biographical Sketches of Distinguished American and Foreign Baptist, and a Supplement.* Philadelphia, Louis H. Everts, 1881; reprint, Paris, AR: Baptist Standard Bearer, 1988.

Encyclopedia of Southern Baptists. S.v. "Pendleton, James Madison," by Leo T. Crismon and Harold Stephens.

BY JOHN FRANKLIN JONES
CORDOVA, TENNESSEE
JULY 2004

THE BAPTIST STANDARD BEARER, INC.

a non-profit, tax-exempt corporation
committed to the Publication & Preservation
of the Baptist Heritage.

CURRENT TITLES AVAILABLE IN
THE BAPTIST *DISTINCTIVES* SERIES

KIFFIN, WILLIAM   A Sober Discourse of Right to Church-Communion. Wherein is proved by Scripture, the Example of the Primitive Times, and the Practice of All that have Professed the Christian Religion: That no Unbaptized person may be Regularly admitted to the Lord's Supper. (London: George Larkin, 1681).

KINGHORN, JOSEPH   Baptism, A Term of Communion. (Norwich: Bacon, Kinnebrook, and Co., 1816)

KINGHORN, JOSEPH   A Defense of "Baptism, A Term of Communion". In Answer To Robert Hall's Reply. (Norwich: Wilkin and Youngman, 1820).

GILL, JOHN   Gospel Baptism. A Collection of Sermons, Tracts, etc., on Scriptural Authority, the Nature of the New Testament Church and the Ordinance of Baptism by John Gill. (Paris, AR: The Baptist Standard Bearer, Inc., 2006).

CARSON, ALEXANDER	Ecclesiastical Polity of the New Testament. (Dublin: William Carson, 1856).
BOOTH, ABRAHAM	A Defense of the Baptists. A Declaration and Vindication of Three Historically Distinctive Baptist Principles. Compiled and Set Forth in the Republication of Three Books. Revised edition. (Paris, AR: The Baptist Standard Bearer, Inc., 2006).
BOOTH, ABRAHAM	Paedobaptism Examined on the Principles, Concessions, and Reasonings of the Most Learned Paedobaptists. With Replies to the Arguments and Objections of Dr. Williams and Mr. Peter Edwards. 3 volumes. (London: Ebenezer Palmer, 1829).
CARROLL, B. H.	*Ecclesia* - The Church. With an Appendix. (Louisville: Baptist Book Concern, 1903).
CHRISTIAN, JOHN T.	Immersion, The Act of Christian Baptism. (Louisville: Baptist Book Concern, 1891).
FROST, J. M.	Pedobaptism: Is It From Heaven Or Of Men? (Philadelphia: American Baptist Publication Society, 1875).
FULLER, RICHARD	Baptism, and the Terms of Communion; An Argument. (Charleston, SC: Southern Baptist Publication Society, 1854).
GRAVES, J. R.	Tri-Lemma: or, Death By Three Horns. The Presbyterian General Assembly Not Able To Decide This Question: "Is Baptism In The Romish Church Valid?" 1st Edition.

	(Nashville: Southwestern Publishing House, 1861).
MELL, P.H.	Baptism In Its Mode and Subjects. (Charleston, SC: Southern Baptist Publications Society, 1853).
JETER, JEREMIAH B.	Baptist Principles Reset. Consisting of Articles on Distinctive Baptist Principles by Various Authors. With an Appendix. (Richmond: The Religious Herald Co., 1902).
PENDLETON, J.M.	Distinctive Principles of Baptists. (Philadelphia: American Baptist Publication Society, 1882).
THOMAS, JESSE B.	The Church and the Kingdom. A New Testament Study. (Louisville: Baptist Book Concern, 1914).
WALLER, JOHN L.	Open Communion Shown to be Unscriptural & Deleterious. With an introductory essay by Dr. D. R. Campbell and an Appendix. (Louisville: Baptist Book Concern, 1859).

For a complete list of current authors/titles, visit our internet site at:
www.standardbearer.org
or write us at:

he Baptist Standard Bearer, Inc.
NUMBER ONE IRON OAKS DRIVE • PARIS, ARKANSAS 72855
TEL # 479-963-3831   FAX # 479-963-8083
EMAIL: Baptist@centurytel.net   http://www.standardbearer.org

Thou hast given a standard to them that fear thee; that it may be displayed because of the truth. — Psalm 60:4

www.ingramcontent.com/pod-product-compliance
Lightning Source LLC
Chambersburg PA
CBHW031310150426
43191CB00005B/169